OPPOSING
VIEWPOINTS®
SERIES

Hacking and Freedom of Information

Other Books of Related Interest

Opposing Viewpoints Series

Cybercrime
Hacking and Hackers
Netiquette and Online Ethics
Whistleblowers

At Issue Series

Cyberpredators
Does the Internet Increase Crime?
Identity Theft
Policing the Internet

Current Controversies Series

Cybercrime
Domestic Surveillance
Espionage and Intelligence
Privacy and Security in the Digital Age

> "Congress shall make no law … abridging the freedom of speech, or of the press."

First Amendment to the US Constitution

The basic foundation of our democracy is the First Amendment guarantee of freedom of expression. The Opposing Viewpoints series is dedicated to the concept of this basic freedom and the idea that it is more important to practice it than to enshrine it.

OPPOSING
VIEWPOINTS®
SERIES

Hacking and Freedom of Information

Marcia Amidon Lusted, Book Editor

GREENHAVEN
PUBLISHING

Published in 2018 by Greenhaven Publishing, LLC
353 3rd Avenue, Suite 255, New York, NY 10010

Copyright © 2018 by Greenhaven Publishing, LLC

First Edition

Articles in Greenhaven Publishing anthologies are often edited for length to meet page
requirements. In addition, original titles of these works are changed to clearly present
the main thesis and to explicitly indicate the author's opinion. Every effort is made to
ensure that Greenhaven Publishing accurately reflects the original intent of the authors.
Every effort has been made to trace the owners of the copyrighted material.

Cover image: gualtiero boffi/Shutterstock.com

Cataloging-in-Publication Data

Names: Lusted, Marcia Amidon, editor.
Title: Hacking and freedom of information / edited by Marcia Amidon Lusted.
Description: New York : Greenhaven Publishing, 2018. | Series: Opposing viewpoints
| Includes bibliographical references and index. | Audience: Grades 9-12.
Identifiers: LCCN ISBN 9781534501782 (library bound) | ISBN 9781534501843 (pbk.)
Subjects: LCSH: Hackers--Juvenile literature. | United States. Freedom of Information
Act--Juvenile literature. | Freedom of information -- United States -- Juvenile literature.
Classification: LCC HV6773.H335 2018 | DDC 364.16/8--dc23

Manufactured in the United States of America

Website: http://greenhavenpublishing.com

Contents

Chapter 1: Why Is Hacking a Concern?

Chapter 2: How Does Hacking Affect the Political Process?

The Importance of Opposing Viewpoints

Perhaps every generation experiences a period in time in which the populace seems especially polarized, starkly divided on the important issues of the day and gravitating toward the far ends of the political spectrum and away from a consensus-facilitating middle ground. The world that today's students are growing up in and that they will soon enter into as active and engaged citizens is deeply fragmented in just this way. Issues relating to terrorism, immigration, women's rights, minority rights, race relations, health care, taxation, wealth and poverty, the environment, policing, military intervention, the proper role of government—in some ways, perennial issues that are freshly and uniquely urgent and vital with each new generation—are currently roiling the world.

If we are to foster a knowledgeable, responsible, active, and engaged citizenry among today's youth, we must provide them with the intellectual, interpretive, and critical-thinking tools and experience necessary to make sense of the world around them and of the all-important debates and arguments that inform it. After all, the outcome of these debates will in large measure determine the future course, prospects, and outcomes of the world and its peoples, particularly its youth. If they are to become successful members of society and productive and informed citizens, students need to learn how to evaluate the strengths and weaknesses of someone else's arguments, how to sift fact from opinion and fallacy, and how to test the relative merits and validity of their own opinions against the known facts and the best possible available information. The landmark series Opposing Viewpoints has been providing students with just such critical-thinking skills and exposure to the debates surrounding society's most urgent contemporary issues for many years, and it continues to serve this essential role with undiminished commitment, care, and rigor.

The key to the series's success in achieving its goal of sharpening students' critical-thinking and analytic skills resides in its title—

Opposing Viewpoints. In every intriguing, compelling, and engaging volume of this series, readers are presented with the widest possible spectrum of distinct viewpoints, expert opinions, and informed argumentation and commentary, supplied by some of today's leading academics, thinkers, analysts, politicians, policy makers, economists, activists, change agents, and advocates. Every opinion and argument anthologized here is presented objectively and accorded respect. There is no editorializing in any introductory text or in the arrangement and order of the pieces. No piece is included as a "straw man," an easy ideological target for cheap point-scoring. As wide and inclusive a range of viewpoints as possible is offered, with no privileging of one particular political ideology or cultural perspective over another. It is left to each individual reader to evaluate the relative merits of each argument—as he or she sees it, and with the use of ever-growing critical-thinking skills—and grapple with his or her own assumptions, beliefs, and perspectives to determine how convincing or successful any given argument is and how the reader's own stance on the issue may be modified or altered in response to it.

This process is facilitated and supported by volume, chapter, and selection introductions that provide readers with the essential context they need to begin engaging with the spotlighted issues, with the debates surrounding them, and with their own perhaps shifting or nascent opinions on them. In addition, guided reading and discussion questions encourage readers to determine the authors' point of view and purpose, interrogate and analyze the various arguments and their rhetoric and structure, evaluate the arguments' strengths and weaknesses, test their claims against available facts and evidence, judge the validity of the reasoning, and bring into clearer, sharper focus the reader's own beliefs and conclusions and how they may differ from or align with those in the collection or those of their classmates.

Research has shown that reading comprehension skills improve dramatically when students are provided with compelling, intriguing, and relevant "discussable" texts. The subject matter of these collections could not be more compelling, intriguing, or urgently relevant to today's students and the world they are poised to inherit. The anthologized articles and the reading and discussion questions that are included with them also provide the basis for stimulating, lively, and passionate classroom debates. Students who are compelled to anticipate objections to their own argument and identify the flaws in those of an opponent read more carefully, think more critically, and steep themselves in relevant context, facts, and information more thoroughly. In short, using discussable text of the kind provided by every single volume in the Opposing Viewpoints series encourages close reading, facilitates reading comprehension, fosters research, strengthens critical thinking, and greatly enlivens and energizes classroom discussion and participation. The entire learning process is deepened, extended, and strengthened.

For all of these reasons, Opposing Viewpoints continues to be exactly the right resource at exactly the right time—when we most need to provide readers with the critical-thinking tools and skills that will not only serve them well in school but also in their careers and their daily lives as decision-making family members, community members, and citizens. This series encourages respectful engagement with and analysis of opposing viewpoints and fosters a resulting increase in the strength and rigor of one's own opinions and stances. As such, it helps make readers "future ready," and that readiness will pay rich dividends for the readers themselves, for the citizenry, for our society, and for the world at large.

Introduction

> *"The vastness of the internet can no longer protect us.... Nowadays, even the most obscure among us can be found by a roving script, and in a startlingly small amount of time."*
>
> —Andrew McGill, *"The Inevitability of Being Hacked,"* The Atlantic, October 28, 2016.

Today we live in a digital age. More and more of the details of everyday life, from banking and business, to communication and social interactions, are taking place online and through computers. Businesses not only need to have their own computer systems, but also need to be connected to other computers and networks to communicate with other businesses. Individuals connect to the world beyond their own laptops and smartphones in order to pay bills, shop, and communicate with others. Computers and the internet have made life easier and faster in many ways, but our increasingly digital world has also brought with it a new set of challenges, especially when it comes to privacy and security. Every connection to the outside world brings with it risks. Hardly a day goes by without news of a new security breach or information leak due to hacking.

What exactly is hacking? The definition of hacking is the process of identifying weaknesses in computer systems or networks, and then using those weaknesses to gain access to the system. This access may allow the hacker to use the information in the system to commit crimes, such as fraud, invasion of privacy and the leaking of private information, and the theft of personal or business information and data. Much of hacking is done for the financial gain of the hacker, but it can also be done maliciously to expose information about a person or corporation to the world, or even just to allow the hacker to "prove" that they can access what might seem like a completely protected computer system or network.

However, in today's world, these definitions of hacking have shifted. Hacking used to have a reputation as an activity done by teenage computer nerds, competing to see who could crack an especially well-guarded computer network. Hacking was also a shadowy activity, done by criminals in order to make money or reveal secrets. But hacking has become a serious activity, done by professionals with extensive knowledge of software and networking systems. Today hacking may be done to expose crimes or secrets and make the world aware of them so that they might be changed. This is a form of activism called "hacktivism." Hacking may also be done to evaluate the security of a computer system of network and identify any possible vulnerabilities, with or without the permission of the network owners. Hacking is also crossing into the territory of freedom of information, with hackers attempting to disclose information from governments or companies which they aren't willing to provide, but which may be important for the general public to know.

Hacking, like many other activities, has its good and bad side. Hacking has a negative reputation because it is so often linked to some sort of theft or invasion of privacy, and can have dire consequences for those people or companies affected by it. But hacking can also be a good thing, such as when it reveals crimes or is used to help strengthen online security. The questions of where and when hacking is a positive thing, and when it is a crime, are controversial. Is it acceptable to use hacking in order to expose or reveal a larger wrongdoing, or force a change? Is hacking allowable in cases where freedom of information is vital? Even though the Freedom of Information Act, first passed into federal law in 1966, does not always guarantee citizens the right to access government information easily or at all. Some citizen groups believe that hacking is the only way to access information that the government does not easily reveal to its people. There are also organizations such as WikiLeaks, which obtain information through hacking and other means, sometimes exposing corruption and secrecy in areas where there should be an open release of information. Is hacking an acceptable activity in cases such as these? Or is it an illegal activity that should not be condoned, even for the greater good?

These are the questions surrounding the issue of hacking, and its related issue, freedom of information. With chapters titled "Why Is Hacking a Concern?" "How Does Hacking Affect the Political Process?" "Are Hackers Criminals?" and "Does the Freedom of Information Act Provide Enough Government Transparency?" *Opposing Viewpoints: Hacking and Freedom of Information* seeks to explore both sides of these issues through the opinions of authors, journalists, and academics who grapple with these questions every day. In a world where more and more of our personal and governmental lives are being regulated or conducted via computers and the internet, they are extremely important questions to consider.

OPPOSING VIEWPOINTS® SERIES

CHAPTER 1

Why Is Hacking a Concern?

Chapter Preface

One of the unresolved questions about hacking is whether or not it should be considered a crime. This is a continuing gray area, since most hacking is still done using unauthorized access and methods that are technically criminal in nature. Yet there are growing instances of hacking being sanctioned by companies and organizations in order to test the strength of their network security measures and identify vulnerabilities in those security systems. Hacking may also be seen as the only way to unearth and reveal the truth about political or corporate dealings that may not be legal in themselves.

A majority of people feel that hacking, as unauthorized access of personal and corporate information, should always be considered illegal. It can cost individuals their privacy as well as rob them economically, and it can cost businesses even more money as well as the confidence of their customers when information is compromised. In this chapter, the viewpoint authors discuss hacking and the need for security and the real costs of cybercrime, but also argue that not all hacking is the same, and not every form of hacking should be considered a crime. Hacking may help identify weaknesses in a system, ultimately leading to better network security. But it can also be a means to conduct espionage between corporations, which can cost companies huge amounts of money. The main question is whether or not all hacking is a crime, and if it can ever be considered to be ethical or even necessary.

> *"Cyber espionage is one of the most important and intriguing international problems in the world today. Understanding this topic is important for understanding how technology shapes the world and influences nation-state relations."*

Cyber Espionage Is Changing the Shape of Modern Warfare

Dana Rubenstein

In the realm of relationships between countries, the act of hacking becomes cyber espionage, or countries spying on each other using computer and network infiltrations. In the following excerpted viewpoint, Dana Rubenstein attempts to define just what cyber espionage is, which countries are using it most frequently, and the tools being used to conduct this type of espionage. Rubenstein also addresses what counter measures may be employed by the countries involved to protect themselves and their information, as well as providing some examples of attempted cyber espionage in recent years and the global significance of these activities. Rubenstein is a specialist, applications developer for AT&T.

"Nation State Cyber Espionage and Its Impacts," by Dana Rubenstein, Washington University in St. Louis, December 1, 2014. Reprinted by permission.

As you read, consider the following questions:

1. According to the Tallinn Manual, what is the definition of cyber espionage?
2. What are some of the tools being used in cyber espionage?
3. What are some of the possible counter-measures to cyber espionage?

Introduction

Cyber espionage is one of the most important and intriguing international problems in world today. Understanding this topic is important for understanding how technology shapes the world and influences nation-state relations. Perhaps the defining feature of cyber espionage is that it occurs in secret, behind the scenes, which unfortunately means that there is a lack of public knowledge about the subject. Details about the "who," "what," and "why" of cyberspace are sometimes unclear, so the following section addresses some of the basic background information about cyber espionage. Even government bodies often have difficulty deciding what constitutes cyber espionage, so the definition is discussed in the first subsection. The second subsection describes current trends in cyber espionage, and the third introduces the nations that are primarily involved in cyber espionage today.

Defining Nation-State Cyber Espionage

One of the most difficult problems regarding cyber warfare is defining cyber espionage. Many nations and international bodies have created their own definitions but it has been difficult to narrow it down to a single consensus. Factors like the extent and nature of the damage caused by the attack, the identity of the attacks, and how the stolen information is used all influence how cyber espionage is perceived. One set of guidelines for nation-state cyber warfare, the Tallinn Manual, attempts to provide definitions, procedures, and rules governing international cyber operations. This manual, published in 2013 as a result of a conference hosted by the NATO Cooperative Cyber Defense Center of Excellence in Tallinn, Estonia, defines cyber espionage as "an act undertaken clandestinely or under false pretenses that uses cyber capabilities to gather (or attempt to gather) information with the intention of communicating it to the opposing party" (Schmitt).

Although most people would characterize cyber espionage as specifically targeting secret information for malicious purposes, this definition does not address the intent of the attack or the nature of the information stolen. This may seem unnecessarily vague but for the purpose of international law this definition is appropriate. At the very minimum it is more helpful for nations that are victims of foreign cyber attacks. Strangely enough, in the modern world it is not technical obstacles, but rather legal and political ones, that make it difficult for nation-states to defend themselves against cyber-attacks. Therefore, an all-encompassing definition of cyber espionage like the one given by the Tallinn Manual is important because it allows victim nations to take appropriate countermeasures for even the slightest intrusion.

Major Powers

Although many countries all over the world are committing cyber espionage, the United States, Russia, and China are considered the most advanced and most prolific cyber spies. Throughout the last decade the United States has started to incorporate cyber warfare into its war doctrine. Preparation first began in 2002 with National Security Presidential Directive 16, which outlined strategies, doctrines, procedures and protocols for cyber warfare. This was followed by the Information Operations Roadmap, published by the Department of Defense in 2003, which started to incorporate cyber warfare preparations, such as training military personnel in cyber defense, as part of normal military operations (Schaap). In 2009, the United States military established the US Cyber Command in Fort Meade, Maryland. The United States is also starting to devote more funding to securing infrastructure that may be vulnerable to cyber-attacks, such as electricity, oil, water, and gas systems (Stone).

Another major player in the cyber espionage game is China. In recent years China has increased the amount of time, resources, and manpower spent on cyber espionage. China's People's Liberation Army, or PLA, includes a special bureau under the intelligence department specifically for cyber intelligence and it enlists programmers right out of college (Stone). According to recent intelligence reports, the PLA is not only capable of advanced surveillance and espionage, but also possesses malware that can take down foreign electricity or water grids (Stone). Though it is usually difficult to confirm the source of any given cyber-attack, according to an October 2011 report to Congress by the United States' National Counterintelligence Executive, it has been confirmed that China is responsible for attacking the United States' networks and stealing secure data in several cases. However, instead of causing outright physical damage, most of China's efforts seem to be on stealing financial and economic secrets in order to build its own economy (McConnell, Chertoff, Lynn).

The final major power in cyber espionage today is Russia. The Russian military is suspected to have cyber weapons more advanced than even China (Paganini 1). Like China, Russia also has special military units dedicated to cyber espionage, where hackers are recruited straight out of university (Stone). However, unlike China, Russia uses its cyber power to supplement more aggressive forms of warfare instead of simply stealing economic secrets. Examples of how Russia has used cyber espionage are discussed below.

[...]

Nation-State Cyber Attacks

Cyber Espionage Tools

Today nation-states employ many different types of cyber espionage tools. Many of these are no different than attacks one might see against one's own home computer, just applied on a much larger scale. First there are DDoS attacks, which are mainly used to disrupt the victim nation-state's communication systems. DDoS attacks are preferred because an attacker can implement them with very limited resources against a larger, more powerful victim. Malware, such as viruses, worms, and Trojan horses, are also popular tools for disrupting normal computer operations, secretly collecting data, or destroying it entirely. Other kinds of attacks include "Logic Bombs", which are malware designed to lie dormant until a specific time or until triggered by a certain event, and IP Spoofing, where an attacker manages to disguise itself in order to gain access to private information or secure networks (Watney). These attacks, while actually common kinds of attacks, can still be devastating if carried out on a large scale by warring nation-states. Also, digital technology is influencing cyber espionage in unexpected ways. Because of advances in photo and video manipulation, once an attacker does gain access to its victim's networks, the attacker can manipulate what the victim is seeing in real time, thus compromising the reliability of the other nation's counterintelligence (Watney).

Recent Attacks

[…]

Cyber espionage does not take place only in the realm of warfare. Nation-states are employing cyber tools against each other to steal economic and financial data as well. As stated above, China seems more interested in using confidential information for economic gain, rather than political advantage. According to United States government reports, thus far the energy, finance, information technology, and automotive industries have experienced attacks originating from China. Commercial industries that have links to military technology and newspapers like *The New York Times*, *The Wall Street Journal*, and *The Washington Post* were also targeted. Most of these attacks are unsuccessful, though many companies do not disclose when they have been attacked, meaning China's success rate could be higher than it appears (Nakashima).

[…]

Defense Strategies

Possible Countermeasures

Deterrence is a useful counter-espionage strategy for nation-states with the authority and the resources to carry it out. Deterrence is when a nation convinces its enemy that it is willing and able to respond to cyber intrusions using military force (Cavelty). The purpose of this is to scare other nation-states from committing cyber attacks in the first place and thus preventing the need for real retaliation. As can be seen Russia's cyber-war victims, the advantage clearly lies in active defense. Of course, when simple deterrence does not work, a nation-state may always resort to retaliating with physical force, but this strategy is very uncommon. As stated above it is often difficult to determine the identity of an attacker, so it would be impractical to waste time and resources on a military operation if a nation was not completely sure of the origin of the attack. Also, according to Article 5 of the UN Charter, defensive force must be "necessary and proportionate to the armed attack that gave rise to the right" (Schaap). No matter how devastating the cyber espionage, it is still difficult for a victim nation to persuade disapproving world powers that deploying troops is an appropriate response to a computer virus.

Perhaps the most effective solution that will be implemented in the future is international cooperation and treaties (Arquilla). Similar to the nuclear arms race, major world powers may eventually recognize that cyber-war is a race without an end and may choose to simply put a stop to it peacefully.

[…]

Impact of Cyber Espionage

Global Significance

Based on the previous section it might seem pretty clear that the impacts of cyber espionage are so severe that of course cyber warfare is something to be concerned about. However, there are some who argue that there is no such thing as "cyber war," or that cyber tools will not affect warfare or daily life in any measurable way. Some analysts believe that cyber war is too disorganized and disjointed for it to be considered a real war (Flynn). Also, it is important to consider the actual probability of such an attack. (Cavelty) argues that because the consequences of cyber espionage can be so harmful, the public perception is that cyber espionage is constantly on the verge of escalating into full-scale war, but in reality, the likelihood of this kind of event is extremely low.

It is also important to consider the impact that politics and media have had on the public perception of cyber espionage. It is likely that politicians would prefer that the perceived threat of cyber war remain high because then they can direct public policy toward combating cyber espionage. Also, when the media reports on cyber espionage it tends to sensationalize it (Cavelty). This is only natural, of course, as they are only looking to sell a good story. But looking at the statistics, in 2010 only about 3% of all cyber intrusions in the United States were so advanced that they could not be stopped. Also, most attackers tend to go after easy targets, like small private companies with data that is not well protected (Cavelty). This means the threat to classified national security information is most likely even lower. Admittedly, this risk does not seem significant.

[…]

More and more countries' infrastructures rely on computer control systems, meaning that they are vulnerable to cyber attacks.

[…]

Even though so far China has only used cyber espionage for economic gain, United States intelligence believes that China's cyber capabilities have reached the level where China is now a national security threat (Stone). Were China to use its power to its full extent, it is unclear whether or not the United States' infrastructure could withstand an attack. This kind of threat shows that cyber war should be taken seriously, and that cyber espionage has deeply impacted modern war and international relations and will likely continue to do so in the future.

References

Dunn Cavelty, Myriam. "The Militarization of Cyberspace: Why Less May Be Better," *IEEE Explore*, 2012 4th International Conference on Cyber Conflict (CYCON), p 1-13.

Watney, Murdoch. "Challenges Pertaining to Cyber War Under International Law," *IEEE Explore*, 2014 Third International Conference on Cyber Security, Cyber Warfare, and Digital Forensics, p 1-5.

Kshetri, Nir. "Cyberwarfare: Western and Chinese Allegations," *IEEE Explore*, IT Professional Vol. 16 Issue 1, p 16-19, 2014.

Arquilla, John. "Cyberwar Is Already Upon Us," Foreign Policy. N.p., 27 Feb. 2012. http://www.foreignpolicy.com/articles/2012/02/27/cyberwar_is_already_upon_us.

Paganini, Pierluigi. "FireEye World War C report—Nation-state driven cyber attacks," Security Affairs RSS., 3 Oct. 2013. http://securityaffairs.co/wordpress/18294/security/fireeye-nation-state-driven-cyber-attacks.html.

Paganini, Pierluigi. "Government Networks Totally Vulnerable to Cyber Attacks," Security Affairs RSS., 18 Feb. 2013. http://securityaffairs.co/wordpress/12312/cyber-crime/government-networks-totally-vulnerable-to-cyber-attacks.html

Paganini, Pierluigi. "Red October, RBN and Too Many Questions Still Unresolved," Security Affairs RSS., 7 Jan. 2013. http://securityaffairs.co/wordpress/11779/cyber-crime/red-october-rbn-and-too-many-questions-still-unresolved.html.

McConnell, Mike, Michael Chertoff, and William Lynn. "China's Cyber Thievery Is National Policy—And Must Be Challenged (2012)," *The Wall Street Journal*, 12 Jan. 2012. http://origin.boozallendr.siteworx.com/content/dam/boozallen/media/file/WSJ-China-OpEd.pdf.

Major Schaap, Arie J. "Cyber Warfare Operations: Development and Use Under International Law," *Cardozo Journal of International and Comparative Law*, Vol 64, p. 121–172. 2009. http://www.afjag.af.mil/shared/media/document/AFD-091026-024.pdf.

Stone, Richard. "A Call to Cyber Arms," *Science Magazine*, Vol 339 Issue 6123, p. 1026-1027. March 1, 2013. http://cryptopenguin.info/cryptome/2013/03/call-to-cyber-arms.pdf.

Nakashima, Ellen. "US Target of Massive Cyber- Espionage Campaign," *The Washington Post*, 10 Feb. 2013. http://www.ctcitraining.org/docs/US_Target_of_Massive_Cyber_Espionage_Campaign.pdf.

Schmitt, Michael N (editor). *Tallinn Manual on the International Law Applicable to Cyber Warfare,* Prepared by the International Group of Experts at the Invitation of the NATO Cooperative Cyber Defence Centre of Excellence. Tallinn, Estonia: International Group of Experts, 2009. Cambridge University Press. NATO Cooperative Cyber Defense Center of Excellence, 2013. http://www.knowledgecommons.in/wp-content/uploads/2014/03/Tallinn-Manual-on-the-International-Law-Applicable-to-Cyber-Warfare-Draft-.pdf.

Weedon, Jen, and Laura Galante. "Intelligence Analysts Dissect the Headlines: Russia, Hackers, Cyberwar! Not So Fast." FireEye Blog., 12 Mar. 2014. http://www.fireeye.com/blog/corporate/2014/03/intel-analysts-dissect-the-headlines-russia-hackers-cyberwar-not-so-fast.html.

Flynn, Matthew J. "Is There a Cyber War?" *Excelsior College, National Cybersecurity Institute Journal*, Vol. 1 Issue 2, p 5-7, 2014.

Wegilant. "What Are Titan Rain Attacks?" Wegilant IT Security Blog., 10 Oct. 2013. http://www.wegilant.com/what-are-titan-rain-attacks/.

Dalziel, Henry. "The Four Amigos: Stuxnet, Flame, Gauss, and DuQu," Concise Courses Security Blog, 2013.

Gragido, Will, John Pirc, and Russ Rogers. *Cybercrime and Espionage: An Analysis of Subversive Multivector Threats*. Rockland, MA: Syngress, 2011.

| *"While the benefits of electronic health records far outweigh the risks, those risks can only be mitigated—not eliminated."*

Our Medical Data Is Vulnerable to Compromise

David Schultz

In the following viewpoint, David Schultz argues that health-care providers should be more protective of their data. With the relatively new advent of digital medical records comes vulnerability to hacking and breaching. When breaches occur, our most private data is exposed. Advocates claim that, unlike financial companies, the health-care industry has been too slow to respond to the challenges unique to digitizing data. But often, health-care providers have been pushed into digitizing their records when they don't have the resources or know-how to protect it. Schultz is a reporter who has worked for Kaiser Health News, NPR, and Bloomberg.

As you read, consider the following questions:

1. What is HIPAA?
2. What constitutes a medical data breach?
3. What suggested methods of securing health records are mentioned in the viewpoint?

"As Patients' Records Go Digital, Theft And Hacking Problems Grow," by David Schultz, Kaiser Family Foundation, June 3, 2012. Reprinted by permission.

A s more doctors and hospitals go digital with medical records, the size and frequency of data breaches are alarming privacy advocates and public health officials.

Keeping records secure is a challenge that doctors, public health officials and federal regulators are just beginning to grasp. And, as two recent incidents at Howard University Hospital show, inadequate data security can affect huge numbers of people.

On May 14, federal prosecutors charged one of the hospital's medical technicians with violating the Health Insurance Portability and Accountability Act, or HIPAA. Prosecutors say that over a 17-month period Laurie Napper used her position at the hospital to gain access to patients' names, addresses and Medicare numbers in order to sell their information. A plea hearing has been set for June 12; Napper's attorney declined comment.

Just a few weeks earlier, the hospital notified more than 34,000 patients that their medical data had been compromised. A contractor working with the hospital had downloaded the patients' files onto a personal laptop, which was stolen from the contractor's car. The data on the laptop was password-protected but unencrypted, which means anyone who guessed the password could have accessed the patient files without a randomly generated key. According to a hospital press release, those files included names, addresses, and Social Security numbers—and, in a few cases, "diagnosis-related information."

Ronald J. Harris, Howard University's top spokesman, said in an email that the two incidents are unrelated, but declined to answer further questions. In its press release about the stolen laptop, the hospital said it will set new requirements for all laptops used by contractors and those issued to hospital personnel to help protect data.

Still it could have been worse. Much worse.

Just days after Howard University contacted its patients about the stolen laptop, the Utah Department of Health announced that hackers based in Eastern Europe had broken into one of

HACK OR ATTACK?

Nearly every day, we see news stories or tweets that reveal another "cyber attack" against a well-known brand, bank or government agency are commonplace today. These are almost always characterized as sophisticated hacking schemes. Some are described as acts of hacktivism. In an effort to characterize certain attacks as the most sophisticated ever, one enthusiastic Wikipedia contributor uses the phrase advanced targeted computer hacking attack. However, the reality is that a cyber attack doesn't necessarily involve hacking, and a great many hacks have nothing to do with attacks.

The term "hack" was originally intended to describe a cleverly written or "coded" piece of software. Often, these kinds of software solved an immediate and thorny problem quickly and efficiently. For example, in the early days of computing, memory was a precious resource, so the developer of a piece of software that made remarkably efficient use of memory might have been complimented as having hacked a great bit of software, and he may have been acknowledged as a terrific hacker. The "hacker" label was a sign of respect. Unfortunately, hacking is now more often associated with cyber attacks, cyber espionage or online criminal activity.

Hacktivism is the use of a cyber attack as a form of protest. Common cyber attacks used by hacktivists are denial of service attacks or website defacements. The term is used very broadly to include attacks against government web sites, law enforcement agencies, online game sites and even terrorist sites... The term hacktivism derives from activism, but many criticize this analog because unlike activists, hacktivists can often attack in the relative safety of the Internet's anonymity.

Are all cyber attacks conducted by hackers? No. Invariably, news and social media channels characterize or glamorize attackers as talented individuals who write very sophisticated software. These characterizations are generally wrong in several respects; while there may be some talented individuals who write crime or attack software, much of what is used as attack software is often not very sophisticated but just clever enough to exploit a vulnerability.

Do all cyber attacks involve hacking? No. Let's use password attacks to illustrate. An attacker who uses social engineering to convince a helpdesk operator to disclose the user name and password for an account does not use a software hack. Such attacks, including some high profile Twitter account and

"Is This A Hack or An Attack?" by Dave Piscitello, Internet Corporation For Assigned Names and Numbers, September 15, 2015.

its servers and stolen personal medical information for almost 800,000 people—more than one of every four residents of the state.

And last November, TRICARE, which handles health insurance for the military, announced that a trove of its backup computer tapes had been stolen from one of its contractors in Virginia. The tapes contained names, Social Security numbers, home addresses and, in some cases, clinical notes and lab test results for nearly 5 million patients, making it the largest medical data breach since the Department of Health and Human Services began tracking incidents two and a half years ago.

As recently as five years ago, it's possible no one outside Howard University would have known about the incidents there. But, new reporting rules adopted as part of the 2009 stimulus act insure the public knows far more about medical data breaches than in the past. When a breach occurs that affects 500 or more patients, health-care providers now must notify not only HHS, but also the media.

Deven McGraw, director of the health privacy project at the Center for Democracy & Technology, a Washington-based internet advocacy group, said the number of incidents is growing with the increased use of digital health records. The health-care industry, she added, has been slow to respond.

"Many financial companies have used encryption for years and they probably wonder what the heck is going on with the health-care industry," McGraw said. "It's much cheaper to deploy safeguards than to suffer a breach."

This growing problem puts HHS in a tough spot. It is pushing hospitals and doctors to adopt electronic health records, but it's also responsible for punishing health-care providers who fail to properly secure their patients' records.

"Mistakes happen, incidents happen, corners get cut from time to time," said Susan McAndrew, deputy director for health information policy at HHS's Office of Civil Rights. "That's where we come in."

What Is a Data Breach?

While a medical data breach can lead to everything from identity theft to billing fraud to blackmail, some breaches ultimately have little consequence on the patients affected. When a medical data breach occurs, it simply means that patient information was, at some point in time, unsecured. For example, in the incident with the Howard University contractor, it's unlikely the person who stole the laptop out of the contractor's car knew—or cared—that there was medical data on it.

According to an HHS database, more than 40 percent of medical data breaches in the past two and a half years involved portable media devices such as laptops or hard drives. McGraw said many of these incidents were entirely avoidable.

"We have technology that can help save us when we're all too human," she said.

Cloud storage, password protection and encryption are all measures health-care providers could be taking to make portable electronic health records more secure, McGraw said.

Another thing that might make health-care providers tighten their security is the potential of facing hefty fines if their patients' data are breached. However, until very recently, providers haven't had to worry much about this.

Since the enactment of HIPAA in 2003 until late last year, there were more than 22,000 complaints about violations of the

Largest Data Breaches

Since 2009, federal law has required health-care providers to report to the Department of Health and Human Services and the news media all data breaches affecting 500 patients or more. These are the top 10 largest medical data breaches since then.

HEALTH-CARE PROVIDER	STATE	PATIENTS AFFECTED	TYPE OF BREACH	DATE
TRICARE	Virginia	4,901,432	Loss of backup tapes	Sept. 13, 2011
Health Net, Inc.	California	1,900,000	Unknown	Jan. 21, 2011
North Bronx Healthcare Network	New York	1,700,000	Electronic medical record theft	Dec. 23, 2010
AvMed, Inc.	Florida	1,220,000	Laptop theft	Dec. 10, 2009
The Nemours Foundation	Florida	1,055,489	Loss of backup tapes	Aug. 10, 2011
Blue Cross Blue Shield of Tennessee	Tennessee	1,023,209	Hard drive theft	Oct. 2, 2009
Sutter Medical Foundation	California	943,434	Desktop computer theft	Oct. 15, 2011
South Shore Hospital	Massachusetts	800,000	Loss of portable electronic device	Feb. 26, 2010
Utah Department of Health	Utah	780,000	Hacking	March 10, 2012 to April 2, 2012
Eisenhower Medical Center	California	514,330	Computer theft	March 11, 2011

Source: U.S. Department of Health and Human Services.

law's privacy rule. HHS issued a monetary penalty only once, according to a report it gave to Congress. Though the department has the power to issue subpoenas when enforcing HIPAA, it has only used that power twice since 2003.

"The industry is very interested and responsive to correct the mistakes that they make and improve their privacy policies," McAndrew said, "so it's not necessary for us to resort to these types of penalties."

Senate Grilling

HHS was criticized for lax enforcement at a Senate hearing in November. In the six months that followed, the department reached settlements in several HIPAA cases with penalties totaling more than $1.5 million.

McGraw said HHS was losing credibility on the enforcement issue, so she's pleased by the department's rapid response to its Senate grilling.

But, she said, federal regulators can only do so much. While the benefits of electronic health records far outweigh the risks, McGraw said, those risks can only be mitigated—not eliminated.

"No matter how good you make the technology," McGraw said, "we'll never get the risk down to zero. But we can do a lot better than we have been doing."

VIEWPOINT 3

> "Relying on inaccurate or unverifiable
> estimates is perilous, experts say,
> because it can tilt the country's
> spending priorities and its relations
> with foreign nations."

How Much Does Cybercrime Cost Us?

Peter Maass and Megha Rajagopalan

*In the following viewpoint, Peter Maass and Megha Rajagopalan
address the question of the financial cost of cybercrime, and whether
it is actually as high as claimed by some major corporations. While
no one would debate that cybercrime does cost companies a great
deal of both money and often consumer faith, does it really result in
trillions of dollars lost? Are these overly high estimates also serving
to exaggerate the true costs of cybercrime and hacking? This is a
concern because government funding to address cybercrimes depends
on accurate assessments. Maass is a senior editor at* The Intercept.
Rajagopalan is a reporter for Buzzfeed World.

"Does Cybercrime Really Cost $1 Trillion?" by Peter Maass and Megha Rajagopalan, *Pro Publica Inc.*, August 1, 2012. Reprinted by permission.

As you read, consider the following questions:

1. How are government officials using cybercrime cost information?
2. Why can it be a challenge to accurately estimate the true cost of cybercrimes?
3. What reasons might companies have for overestimating the costs of cybercrime?

G en. Keith Alexander is the director of the National Security Agency and oversees U.S. Cyber Command, which means he leads the government's effort to protect America from cyberattacks. Due to the secretive nature of his job, he maintains a relatively low profile, so when he does speak, people listen closely. On July 9, Alexander addressed a crowded room at the American Enterprise Institute in Washington, D.C., and though he started with a few jokes—his mother said he had a face for radio, behind every general is a stunned father-in-law—he soon got down to business.

Alexander warned that cyberattacks are causing "the greatest transfer of wealth in history," and he cited statistics from, among other sources, Symantec Corp. and McAfee Inc., which both sell software to protect computers from hackers. Crediting Symantec, he said the theft of intellectual property costs American companies $250 billion a year. He also mentioned a McAfee estimate that the global cost of cybercrime is $1 trillion. "That's our future disappearing in front of us," he said, urging Congress to enact legislation to improve America's cyberdefenses.

These estimates have been cited on many occasions by government officials, who portray them as evidence of the threat against America. They are hardly the only cyberstatistics used by officials, but they are recurring ones that get a lot of attention. In his first major cybersecurity speech in 2009, President Obama prominently referred to McAfee's $1 trillion estimate. Sen. Joseph Lieberman, I-Conn., and Sen. Susan Collins, R-Maine, the main sponsors of the Cybersecurity Act of 2012 that is expected to be voted on this week, have also mentioned $1 trillion in cybercrime costs. Last week, arguing on the Senate floor in favor of putting their bill up for a vote, they both referenced the $250 billion estimate and repeated Alexander's warning about the greatest transfer of wealth in history.

A handful of media stories, blog posts and academic studies have previously expressed skepticism about these attention-getting estimates, but this has not stopped an array of government officials and politicians from continuing to publicly cite them as authoritative. Now, an examination of their origins by *ProPublica* has found new grounds to question the data and methods used to generate these numbers, which McAfee and Symantec say they stand behind.

One of the figures Alexander attributed to Symantec—the $250 billion in annual losses from intellectual property theft—was indeed mentioned in a Symantec report, but it is not a Symantec number and its source remains a mystery.

McAfee's trillion-dollar estimate is questioned even by the three independent researchers from Purdue University whom McAfee credits with analyzing the raw data from which the estimate was derived. "I was really kind of appalled when the number came out in news reports, the trillion dollars, because that was just way, way large," said Eugene Spafford, a computer science professor at Purdue.

Spafford was a key contributor to McAfee's 2009 report, "Unsecured Economies: Protecting Vital Information". The trillion-dollar estimate was first published in a news release that McAfee issued to announce the report; the number does not appear in the report itself. A McAfee spokesman told *ProPublica* the estimate was an extrapolation by the company, based on data from the report. McAfee executives have mentioned the trillion-dollar figure on a number of occasions, and in 2011 McAfee published it once more in a new report, "Underground Economies: Intellectual Capital and Sensitive Corporate Data Now the Latest Cybercrime Currency."

In addition to the three Purdue researchers who were the report's key contributors, 17 other researchers and experts were listed as contributors to the original 2009 report, though at least some of them were only interviewed by the Purdue researchers. Among them was Ross Anderson, a security engineering professor at University of Cambridge, who told *ProPublica* that he did not know about the $1 trillion estimate before it was announced. "I would have objected at the time had I known about it," he said. "The intellectual quality of this ($1 trillion number) is below abysmal."

The use of these estimates comes amid increased debate about cyberattacks; warnings of a digital Pearl Harbor are becoming almost routine. "A cyberattack could stop our society in its tracks," Gen. Martin Dempsey, chairman of the Joint Chiefs of Staff, said earlier this year. Bloomberg reported just last week that a group of Chinese hackers, whom U.S. intelligence agencies referred to as "Byzantine Candor," have stolen sensitive or classified information from 20 organizations, including Halliburton Inc., and a prominent Washington law firm, Wiley Rein LLP.

There is little doubt that a lot of cybercrime, cyberespionage and even acts of cyberwar are occurring, but the exact scale is unclear and the financial costs are difficult to calculate because solid data is hard to get. Relying on inaccurate or unverifiable estimates is perilous, experts say, because it can tilt the country's spending priorities and its relations with foreign nations. The costs could be worse than the most dire estimates—but they could be less, too.

Computer security companies like McAfee and Symantec have stepped into the data void. Both sell anti-virus software to consumers, and McAfee also sells a range of network security products for government agencies and private companies, including operators of critical infrastructure like power plants and pipelines. Both firms conduct and publish cybercrime research, too. "Symantec is doing outstanding work on threat analysis," said Thomas Rid, a cybersecurity expert at Kings College London. "But still, of course they have a vested interest in portraying a more dangerous environment because they stand to gain for it."

The companies disagree. Sal Viveros, a McAfee public relations official who oversaw the 2009 report, said in an email to *ProPublica*, "We work with think tanks and universities to make sure our reports are non-biased and as accurate as possible. The goal of our papers [is] to really educate on the issues and risks facing businesses. Our customers look to us to provide them with our expert knowledge."

Symantec said its estimates are developed with standard methods used by governments and businesses to conduct consumer surveys and come from "one of the few, large, multi-country studies on cybercrime that asks consumers what forms of cybercrime they have actually experienced and what it cost them."

Cyberattacks come in many flavors. There are everyday crimes in which hackers access personal or financial information, such as credit card numbers. There are industrial crimes and espionage in which the attacker—perhaps a foreign country or company—breaks into a corporate or government network to obtain blueprints or classified information; sometimes the attacker gets inside a network and lurks there for months or years, scooping up whatever is of interest. One of the biggest categories of cybercrime is one of the least discussed—insider theft, by disgruntled or ex-employees. There's also a category of attacks that do not have overt financial motives and that can constitute acts of war: Attempts to create havoc in computer systems that control nuclear power plants, dams and the electrical grid. This category is of the greatest concern to national security officials.

One reason it's a challenge to measure the financial costs of cybercrimes is that the victims often don't know they've been attacked. When intellectual property is stolen, the original can remain in place, seemingly untouched. Even when the breach is known, how do you put a dollar value on a Social Security number, a formula for a new drug, the blueprints for a new car, or the bidding strategy of an oil firm? It may be impossible to know whether an attacker uses intellectual property in a way that causes economic harm to the victim; maybe the data isn't of much use to the attacker, or maybe the attacker, though using the data to quickly bring out a new product, is not successful in gaining market share.

There's an added complication in some attacks: Companies can be reluctant to admit they have been hacked because they fear a loss in confidence from consumers or clients. This can lead to underreporting of the problem.

"How do you even start to measure the monetary damages?" asked Nick Akerman, a partner at the law firm of Dorsey & Whitney LLP who specializes in computer cases—and one of the contributors to the McAfee report. "I would argue it is impossible. Not to say the problem isn't enormous. It is enormous. But I don't see how you can adequately come up with dollar figures."

Companies that sell security software are not bound by the same professional practices as academics, whose studies tend to refrain from sweeping estimates. Even when corporate reports involve academic researchers, the results can be suspect. Industry-sponsored studies—pharmaceuticals are an example, according to a 2003 study published by BMJ (formerly known as the British Medical Journal)—can have a bias toward the industry's economic interests. Unlike academic journals, which use a peer review process, there's no formal system of oversight for studies published by industry. The economic interest of security companies is clear: The greater the apparent threat, the greater the reason to buy their anti-intruder software. Norton, which is owned by Symantec and sells a popular suite of anti-virus software, advises in its latest cybercrime report: "Don't get angry. Get Norton."

Computer scientists Dinei Florencio and Cormac Herley, who work at Microsoft Research, the software giant's computer science lab, recently wrote a paper, "Sex, Lies and Cyber-crime Surveys," that sharply criticized these sorts of surveys. "Our assessment of the quality of cyber-crime surveys is harsh: they are so compromised and biased that no faith whatever can be placed in their findings," their report said. "We are not alone in this judgement. Most research teams who have looked at the survey data on cyber-crime have reached similarly negative conclusions."

Julie Ryan, a professor of engineering management and systems engineering at George Washington University, co-authored a paper, "The Use, Misuse, and Abuse of Statistics in Information Security Research". In an interview with *ProPublica*, she said: "From what I've seen of the big commercial surveys, they all suffer from major weaknesses, which means the data is worthless, scientifically worthless. But it's very valuable from a marketing perspective."

Yet corporate cybersurveys are repeatedly invoked; the NSA's Alexander is merely among the most prominent senior officials to do it. *ProPublica* provided the NSA's media office with links to critical studies, stories and blog posts about the Symantec and McAfee numbers and asked whether Alexander or the agency was aware of them or, alternately, had other data to support the numbers he cited. The NSA media office responded: "The information is publicly available and was appropriately sourced."

McAfee was founded by John McAfee, a software engineer who wrote some of the first anti-virus software in the 1980s. The company grew quickly, thanks in part to a novel marketing strategy in those days—McAfee gave away its software, charging only for tech support. The company went public in 1992 and remained a leader in its field; last year it was acquired by Intel Corp. for $7.68 billion. "We have had just one mission: to help our customers stay safe," McAfee says on its website. "We achieve this by creating proactive security solutions for securing your digital world."

In 2008, McAfee decided to commission a report that would look at how the global economic downturn was affecting data theft against companies. McAfee put one of its public relations officials, Viveros, in charge of the project. Viveros, in a phone interview, said a technology marketing company was hired to create and distribute a survey to about 1,000 information and technology executives across the globe. Purdue University's Center for Education and Research in Information Assurance and Security, headed by Spafford, analyzed the survey results, conducted follow-up interviews and helped write the report. McAfee confirmed that it helped steer $30,000 from a foundation to Purdue for the work.

The 31-page report found that the companies surveyed had an average of $12 million worth of sensitive information stored in offshore computer systems in 2008, and that each lost an average $4.6 million worth of intellectual property in 2008. The report was released on Jan. 29, 2009, in Davos, Switzerland, during a meeting of the World Economic Forum. McAfee issued a news release to announce it, and the release included dramatic numbers that were not in the report.

"The companies surveyed estimated they lost a combined $4.6 billion worth of intellectual property last year alone, and spent approximately $600 million repairing damage from data breaches," the release said. "Based on these numbers, McAfee projects that companies worldwide lost more than $1 trillion last year." The release contained a quote from McAfee's then-president and chief executive David DeWalt, in which he repeated the $1 trillion estimate. The headline of the news release was "Businesses Lose More than $1 Trillion in Intellectual Property Due to Data Theft and Cybercrime."

The trillion-dollar estimate was picked up by the media, including Bloomberg and CNET, which expressed no skepticism. But at least one observer had immediate doubts. Amrit Williams, a security consultant, wrote on his blog a few days later, "$1 trillion a year? Seriously? Where the hell did the figure come from? To give you some perspective of size the total US GDP is about 14 trillion and that includes EVERYTHING."

The news stories got the worried attention of some of the report's contributors because McAfee was connecting their names to an estimate they had no previous knowledge of and were skeptical about. One of the contributors, Augusto Paes de Barros, a Brazilian security consultant, blogged a week after the news release that although he was glad to have been involved in the report, "I could not find any data in that report that could lead into that number. ... I'd like to see how they found this number."

When the number was announced in 2009, McAfee provided no public explanation of how it was derived. "Initially we were just going to do the report, but a lot of people were asking us what was the total number, so we worked on a model," said McAfee's Viveros. This week, in response to queries from *ProPublica*, he disclosed details about the methodology. He said the calculations were done by a group of technology, marketing and sales officials at McAfee and were based on the survey responses.

"McAfee extrapolated the $1 trillion...based on the average data loss per company, multiplied by the number of similar companies in the countries we studied," Viveros said in an email.

The company's method did not meet the standards of the Purdue researchers whom it had engaged to analyze the survey responses and help write the report. In phone interviews and emails to *ProPublica*, associate professor Jackie Rees Ulmer said she was disconcerted when, a few days before the report's unveiling, she received a draft of the news release that contained the $1 trillion figure. "I expressed my concern with the number as we did not generate it," Rees Ulmer said in an email. She added that although she couldn't recall the particulars of the phone conversation in which she made her concerns known, "It is almost certainly the case that I would have told them the number was unsupportable."

Viveros said McAfee was never told by Purdue that the number could not be supported by the survey data. The company moved ahead with the news release and, Viveros noted, the trillion-dollar estimate "got a life of its own."

In February 2009, President Obama ordered a 60-day cybersecurity review to look into ways to better protect the country from cyberattacks, and he appointed Melissa Hathaway, who served as a cybersecurity adviser in the Bush administration, to oversee the effort. On May 29, Obama unveiled the review and delivered his first major cybersecurity speech. The second page of the 38-page review cited McAfee's trillion-dollar figure, and the president used it in his speech, saying, "It's been estimated that last year alone cybercriminals stole intellectual property from businesses worldwide worth up to $1 trillion."

The administration's Cyberspace Policy Review includes footnotes, and the one for the $1 trillion estimate directs readers to McAfee's news release. It is not an ordinary occurrence that a president relies on the contents of a corporate news release to warn Americans of a major threat to the homeland's economic and national security, but Hathaway, now a security consultant, told *ProPublica* that at the time of the president's speech she was comfortable with McAfee's estimate because it appeared to be associated with Purdue researchers. However, she became wary of it once she began making more inquiries after the speech. "I tend not to use that number anymore," she said. "I was surprised that there wasn't proved methodology behind the number."

In March 2011, McAfee published its "Underground Economies" report, which repeated the $1 trillion estimate. Criticism of it continued, too. Robert Richardson, then director of the Computer Security Institute, skeptically wrote on the group's website in the spring of 2011 that "The trillion dollar number is just too good to kill." Later in 2011, *Wired*'s British edition reported that "if true, the figure amounts to a massive 1.6 percent of global GDP." This year, Microsoft Research's Florencio and Herley wrote an opinion piece in *The New York Times* that described widely circulated cybercrime estimates as "generated using absurdly bad statistical methods, making them wholly unreliable."

These critiques have now taken on added importance because government officials are citing a variety of industry-generated numbers in their efforts to bolster support for major cybersecurity legislation. The House passed its version of a cybersecurity bill this spring; the pending Senate bill, known as the Cybersecurity Act of 2012, would enable the U.S. government and private companies to more easily share information about cyberthreats and create a set of voluntary cybersecurity standards for operators of critical infrastructure.

In his speech at the American Enterprise Institute, Gen. Alexander said Symantec placed the cost of intellectual property theft to the U.S. at $250 billion a year. Tracing the origins of this statistic—as both the U.S. Government Accountability Office and technology writer Julian Sanchez have attempted before—is not unlike pulling a piece of yarn to unravel an old sweater. Although Symantec mentioned the $250 billion estimate in a 2011 report, "Behavioral Risk Indicators of IP Theft," the estimate is not Symantec's.

The report mentions the figure in passing, sourcing it in a footnote to a legal paper, where, as it turns out, the $250 billion number is not mentioned at all. Eric Shaw, one of two forensic psychologists Symantec retained to research the "Behavioral Risk" report, told *ProPublica* the footnote was a mistake. Instead, it should have referred to a different paper that points to a 2003 speech by FBI Director Robert S. Mueller. The figure is also cited in old FBI news releases available via the Internet Archive.

An agency spokeswoman said that although she believed FBI officials used a reliable source for the number, the FBI had neither developed the number nor claimed to have done so. She pointed to another document, from the U.S. Department of Justice, attributing the $250 billion figure to the Office of the U.S. Trade Representative.

Then-Commerce Secretary Gary Locke used the $250 billion number in a 2010 speech. Like Locke, the trade representative is a member of the president's cabinet; a spokeswoman for the office said the figure was not from them. "Your inquiry appears to refer to an industry-reported figure," the spokeswoman told *ProPublica*, pointing to a U.S. Chamber of Commerce paper on intellectual property theft. Sure enough, there's the $250 billion again—this time attributed to none other than the FBI.

There are other concerns about Symantec estimates cited by Alexander. Drawing from the 2011 Norton Cybercrime Report, Alexander put the direct cost of cybercrime at $114 billion and cybercrime's total cost, factoring in time lost, at $388 billion.

The report was not actually researched by Norton employees; it was outsourced to a market research firm, StrategyOne, which is owned by the public relations giant Edelman.

StrategyOne surveyed almost 20,000 people in 24 countries, asking them to report whether they had experienced cybercrime and how much it had cost them. The company said it used "standard research practice for online surveys" to obtain a representative sample of internet users. To calculate a total cost, it multiplied the estimated number of victims by the average cost of cybercrime in each country.

But that still leaves room for uncertainty, several researchers told *ProPublica*. For example, if responses came mainly from those most concerned about cybercrime or from those who suffered the biggest losses, it could inflate the average cost. And one person's estimate of the financial damage from a cybercrime might be completely different from the next person's guess, even if both suffered the same crime and the same amount of lost time.

A StrategyOne spokesman, asked if the Symantec estimates could be called scientific, responded, "Yes, as much as any survey or poll that relies on consumers to estimate their losses based on recall."

Some experts say that's not good enough. "Nobody can really assess the true impact of cybercrime," said Franz-Stefan Gady, an analyst at a security-focused think tank called the EastWest Institute. "It's really the self-reporting—because we can't verify it. It's just as simple as that."

In their 2011 paper, Florencio and Herley of Microsoft Research did not specifically mention the Symantec or McAfee numbers. But they observed, "Far from being broadly-based estimates of losses across the population, the cyber-crime estimates that we have appear to be largely the answers of a handful of people extrapolated to the whole population."

Sen. Collins added another layer of confusion about the mysterious $250 billion figure when she spoke last week in support of the cybersecurity bill. In remarks on the Senate floor, she mentioned Gen. Alexander and said, "He believes American companies have lost about $250 billion a year through intellectual property theft."

Collins' office declined several requests for comment. A spokeswoman for Lieberman, who similarly cited Alexander and the $250 billion figure, replied, "Senator Lieberman and his staff believe that McAfee, Symantec, and General Alexander are reputable sources of information about cybersecurity."

> *"If the information falls into the wrong hands, it could be beyond damaging."*

It Is Essential to Protect Systems Against Hackers

G.C. Eric Brumfield

In the following viewpoint, G.C. Eric Brumfield argues that in today's world, information equals power and money, and so it must be protected. This will require increasingly sophisticated measures to safeguard this information. Brumfield explores some of the proactive, internal, and external measures that can be taken by businesses to protect their information, as well as where technology is heading and how companies will have to continually adapt their security. Brumfield is president of BIT Consultants Incorporated, an IT Staffing Firm in Detroit, Michigan.

As you read, consider the following questions:

1. Why do businesses need to safeguard their computer systems?
2. What can businesses do to prevent hacking attacks before they happen?
3. What are some of the things that hackers do to businesses that they gain access to?

As our world heads into the next millennium, companies in every industry are becoming more computer literate. Their need for some level of sophisticated networks to keep their competitive edge is becoming greater. With every network that is installed in an organization, there is also a risk that proper security measures were overlooked or taken for granted. In these cases, companies can face a great deal of embarrassment and anxiety and even lose millions of dollars due to security breaches.

When should companies invest in security systems? When can they determine if they are at risk without one? A rule of thumb is, any company that routinely stores sensitive, confidential information that is critical to their success, or information that could cause damage to them were it to end up in the wrong hands, should definitely look for a sound security system to protect its investment. Companies utilizing a local area network with a small number of users are at a lower risk than those that utilize a wide area network that connects to multiple sites within a city or multiple sites throughout the country.

Information equates to power and money in this day and age. The internet is becoming one of the fastest ways to start a new business, grow an existing business or simply find needed information. Jim Reed, manager of public relations for V-One, a network security company in Germantown, Maryland, says, "It's business-to-business commerce through the internet that is going to make the internet even bigger than it is now. And with companies communicating with each other through the internet, vital information is being transferred back and forth. If the information falls into the wrong hands, it could be beyond damaging."

Law offices and other industries have to deal with the power of confidentiality. As we take a closer look at how freely information is passed via our internal networks and the internet, we must begin to recognize the importance of having an adequate network security system that will protect this information and secure the rights of confidentiality for businesses and our clients.

CYBER-HACKING IN CORPORATE ESPIONAGE

Hackers believed to have originated in China compromised at least five multinational oil and energy companies in "coordinated covert and targeted" cyberattacks, according to a report by cybersecurity firm McAfee.

The network intrusions, which have been dubbed "Night Dragon" by McAfee, are believed to have begun in November 2009...

"This is a breed of attackers that are interested in industrial or national-security espionage," said Dmitri Alperovitch, vice president of threat research at McAfee Labs. "Their primary characteristic and differentiator from cybercriminals is that they are persistent. Like a dog with a bone, they just don't let go of their victim."

The report states the attacks are continuing.

Operating from a base apparently in Beijing, the intruders established control servers in the United States and Netherlands to break into computers in Kazakhstan, Taiwan, Greece, and the United States, according to the report...

"As McAfee notes, the attack techniques in Night Dragon are old—[about] a decade old—and industrial espionage via computer networks is also well-known," said Chris Palmer, technology director for the Electronic Frontier Foundation.

This is good news for those tasked with detecting and preventing attacks, Palmer said. "The attacks have used mostly old and well-understood attack techniques."

For example, Palmer says there are good defenses against the spear-phishing technique used in the Night Dragon attacks. Spear-phishing refers to attempts to retrieve usernames, passwords, and other sensitive information through emails that appear to come from a trusted source.

Palmer noted spear-phishing is likely to work well for a long time.

"Confusing people and impersonating their friends works very well on the Internet, unfortunately," Palmer said of spear-phishing.

Palmer warned, "Defense techniques only work if software engineers are motivated or required to use them. We had a brief period of forward momentum on security engineering from about 2004 through 2009, but I fear we are losing that momentum."

Despite Palmer's assertion spear-phishing attacks are easily defended against, Alperovitch says it's difficult to deter and prevent attack techniques such as the ones used in Night Dragon.

"At the end of the day, there is nothing you can really do to deter attacks like these. The best you can hope for is to detect the infiltration activity fast enough to block it and prevent catastrophic data loss," he said.

"It is a never-ending, vigilant fight with a very determined and resourceful attacker," he said.

"Cyber-Hacking Is Latest Tool in Corporate Espionage," by Alyssa Carducci, Heartland Institute, May 31, 2016.

Proactive Measures

After accomplishing the great task of installing a network security system, there is yet another concern that demands close attention: the ability to manage network security systems effectively so that hackers do not break through security walls and create nightmares for us all. Hacker is more than just a word to many. For some it's, a career, and for others it is like a vampire in the night waiting to suck the blood and money from the life of a company. Most organizations in business today have been the victim of hackers at one time or another. Part of the reason is that hackers come in many shapes and sizes. They can be as small and as brilliant as the adolescent genius that lives next door–the kid that spends his time solving puzzles and breaking passwords on his PC in the basement, instead of playing with the boring computer-illiterate kids in the neighborhood. Or hackers can be as dangerous as the professionals, known as "Black Hats," computer criminals who make a living by breaking into unsuspecting computer systems and selling, destroying or manipulating data or information they poach.

How can businesses protect their investments with criminals waiting for the perfect opportunity to penetrate security systems? There are many security measures that can be taken. Some are very small steps, and others involve financial investments.

One major step that organizations can take is to eliminate use of the internet on the job. It is common knowledge that internet access and a modem are key sources of entry into an organization's computer system. And every organization has its workaholics—you know, people who are so dedicated to work that they have to take some of it home with them. Then they remotely access the server at the office to make modifications to their critical projects. If the firewalls of our network security systems allow people with just average computer literacy to enter, then what opportunities for intrusion exist for the "Black Hats" of the world. Just a simple password can create a virtual playground for the professional hacker.

Welcome to the world of hacker. According to the third annual "Computer Crime and Security Survey," conducted by the Computer Security Institute in San Francisco (http:www.gocsi. com), computer crime and other information security breaches are on the rise, and the cost to U.S. corporations and government agencies is growing.

The CSI report released last March noted that 64 percent of respondents reported computer security breaches within the last year. This figure is 16 percent higher than CSI's 1997 survey.

CSI also reported that, although most organizations have firewalls in place at their network perimeters, more than 70 percent had security flaws which left them vulnerable to even the most rudimentary malicious attacks.

Internal Measures

Companies must first take proactive measures from within. Initial steps should block the curious onlooker or the average computer hacker. This would basically protect documents within the system from internal onlookers, but it will not protect them from that experienced hacker outside, looking in. Measures might include password protection, masking and information-change detection. Getting into the habit of changing passwords regularly is a wise thing to do.

It's recommended that companies change user passwords at least once a quarter. Masking techniques include disguising files inside the computer, or hiding ranges of information inside a file to make information appear unreadable or invisible. Change-detection techniques include audit trails such as byte count and formula difference locators. There are many security programs available in today's marketplace that address spreadsheet and word-processing techniques, operating systems security, database protection, and general safeguards and internet security, to name just a few. Depending on your business, any one or all of these programs would benefit to the protection of data or information within your systems. Companies that implement such internal protective measures move one step closer to preventing incidents like the Bernard Mayles case in 1991. Bernard stole drug-processing information from his then-employer pharmaceuticals giant Merck & Co, and tried to peddle it to an Eastern European company. That company's agent turned out to have a different employer: the FBI. Mayles was sentenced to nine years in prison.

Another situation that might have been avoided is the case of a retail store chain managed by Bill Kesl, director of systems integration at Datamax Systems Solutions in Boca Raton, Florida. A computer-savvy store clerk at Kesl's would log on to an electronic register and change prices so that an accomplice could buy items for next to nothing. In both cases, individuals were able to access sensitive computer information and use it for dishonest purposes, due to relaxed security parameters.

External Measures

As companies move toward decentralized networks of personal computers and away from centralized, easily protected mainframes, they become more vulnerable to hacking. In an effort to make businesses more user-friendly, we are inevitably making them more hacker-friendly as well.

The "Black Hats" of the world create varied nightmares for businesses. A hacker tampered with automaker BMW's website as a

New Year's prank last January, taking the image of a BMW roadster tearing down the highway and transforming it into a car wreck by turning the car upside down and painting in skid marks. Later that same month, critics of Indonesia's then-President Suharto hit 15 government domains, including the site of the nation's police force, inserting their views onto the websites.

There is also the "denial of service" attack, in which a hacker tricks a computer so that it shuts down or is so busy with bogus requests that it can't handle legitimate ones. In March, a series of "denial of service" attacks crippled hundreds of systems, including computers owned by NASA and other government agencies, various academic institutions, Microsoft Corporation and other commercial institutions. Last year a virus shut down computers for two days at National City Corporation, a Cleveland bank. The bank spent at least $400,000 to correct the virus rewiring during the attack to activate backup computers.

In a survey conducted last year by Information Week and Ernst & Young of New York, 40 percent of respondents reported losses of up to $100,000 from macro viruses; nearly half (47 percent) reported losses of up to $100,000 due to other types of viruses.

Nick Simicich, an IBM Senior Security consultant in Boca Raton, Florida, tests social engineering methods when conducting security audits for clients. Social Engineering is a term that commonly used by low-key hackers to describe posing as employees of a company in order to gain sensitive information. "I've gone up to a security person carrying a laptop," Simicich says, "asked him what the policy is on laptops and walked out the door." He has also gotten passwords by posing as a company computer technician: "I'll just say, 'Could you do me a favor and give me your password so I don't have to look it up?'" These are just a few of the potentially hundreds of techniques that hackers use to wreak havoc on our organizations.

One very common preventive measure that companies are using is to hire outside organizations to strengthen their network security systems. The organizations conduct a series of diagnostic tests from outside, to see how easy it is to crack the firewalls of the target organization—with the permission of the organization. This adds a new twist, paying someone to hack systems to discover the weaknesses.

One company that provides this service to all industries is IBM. Dave Gamey, of IBM Canada, is a consultant for public and private-sector organizations, including banks. Gamey is engaged in an ongoing war against computer criminals as a member of a 100-man team of "White Hats." The White Hats charge up to $40,000 to attempt to outwit their black-hatted opponents, using technologies such as Trojan horses, jails, spoofing, password guessers, war-dialers, stealth port scanners, firewalls, sniffers, daemons and finger commands. When Gamey and his team win, they can save a company embarrassment, anxiety, hours of labor costs and millions of dollars in potential losses. The $40,000 cost for this service is minimal; Gamey and his merry team of white hatters believe that they have saved millions for their clients.

Where Are We Heading

Traditionally, computer crimes have been inside jobs. But technology continues to advance, giving us all the potential to gain a competitive edge. Companies need take the proper steps to avoid internal hacking and to set security parameters, because it will become increasingly more expensive to secure data. John D. Spain, executive vice president of information technology security at Asset Management Solutions, an Atlanta-based security firm, says, "Companies need to classify their information. If you don't know what you need to protect, it's hard to protect it." We must all become more knowledgeable about common occurrences of internal and external hacking in our types of businesses, to protect our investments better in the next millennium.

Network Security Systems are a great enough problem by itself. One that has the government setting regulations on the use of information flowing through the internet with encryptions on it. Today our worry is the loss of great profits as a result of this hacker problem, let's hope that tomorrow our worry won't be that we will all be living in a world like the one depicted in the 1998 movie, "Enemy of the State," where the government is the real "Black Hat" to worry about.

Once we take the time and make the necessary investments to determine our security needs we will move one step closer to what we would all like to believe is "real security."

Periodical and Internet Sources Bibliography

The following articles have been selected to supplement the diverse views presented in this chapter.

"A large-scale cyber-attack highlights the structural dilemma of the NSA." *The Economist*, May 13, 2017. https://www.economist.com/news/science-and-technology/21722026-americas-national-security-agency-torn-between-defending-computer-systems-and.

Bradley K. Ashley, "The United States Is Vulnerable to Cyberterrorism." *AFCEA International*, March 2004. https://www.afcea.org/content/?q=node/32.

"Computer Crime Statutes." *National Conference of State Legislatures*, December 5, 2016. http://www.ncsl.org/research/telecommunications-and-information-technology/computer-hacking-and-unauthorized-access-laws.aspx.

"Cyber Warfare: Hype and Fear." *The Economist*, December 8, 2012. https://www.economist.com/news/international/21567886-america-leading-way-developing-doctrines-cyber-warfare-other-countries-may.

Clare Edwards, "Is Computer Hacking a Crime?" *It Still Works*, accessed August 8, 2017. http://itstillworks.com/computer-hacking-crime-1387.html.

"History of FOIA." *Electronic Frontier Foundation*. https://www.eff.org/issues/transparency/history-of-foia.

David M. Hafele, "Three Different Shades of Ethical Hacking: Black, White and Gray." *SANS Institute*, February 23, 2004. https://www.sans.org/reading-room/whitepapers/hackers/shades-ethical-hacking-black-white-gray-1390.

Kevin Maney, "Can Hackers Be Stopped? The State of Defense in the Private Sector." *Newsweek*, November 2, 2016. http://www.newsweek.com/2016/11/11/war-against-hacking-cyber-crime-515935.html.

"Medical Identity Theft in Healthcare," *Secure Technology Alliance*, March 2010. https://www.securetechalliance.org/publications-medical-identity-theft-in-healthcare/.

Jose Pagliery, "The Evolution of Hacking." *CNN*, June 5, 2015. http://www.cnn.com/2015/03/11/tech/computer-hacking-history/index.html.

Paul Wagenseil, "How computer hacking laws make you a criminal." *NBC News*, January 17, 2013. http://www.nbcnews.com/tech/security/how-computer-hacking-laws-make-you-criminal-f1B8022563.

M. Mitchell Waldrop, "How to Hack the Hackers: The Human Side of Cyber Crime." *Nature Magazine*, May 12, 2016. https://www.scientificamerican.com/article/how-to-hack-the-hackers-the-human-side-of-cyber-crime/.

Matthew Weaver, "Teenage hackers motivated by morality not money, study finds." *The Guardian*, April 21, 2017. https://www.theguardian.com/society/2017/apr/21/teenage-hackers-motivated-moral-crusade-money-cybercrime.

"What is Hacking? Introduction & Types." *Guru 99*, 2017. https://www.guru99.com/what-is-hacking-an-introduction.html.

"What We Investigate: Cyber Crime." *Federal Bureau of Investigation*. Accessed August 8, 2017. https://www.fbi.gov/investigate/cyber.

"Who Are Hackers?" *PBS Frontline*. Accessed August 8, 2017. http://www.pbs.org/wgbh/pages/frontline/shows/hackers/whoare/.

OPPOSING
VIEWPOINTS®
SERIES

CHAPTER 2

How Does Hacking Affect the Political Process?

Chapter Preface

One of the biggest issues surrounding the 2016 US presidential election and its aftermath has been the involvement of Russia in the political process, and whether Russia interfered in the outcome of the election using hacking and other methods. The US government publicly announced that it was "confident" that Russia was behind the email hacking attacks on the Democratic National Committee (DNC) and other Democratic organizations. The result was the release of thousands of stolen emails with content that damaged candidate Hillary Clinton and the Democratic Party. While an investigation has been started into these allegations and the possible corruption of the election process, and no firm conclusions have yet been reached, the issue has brought hacking into the spotlight even more than usual. The idea that the elections of the United States government could be swayed or corrupted by an outside party, such as another country or political party, has made many people wonder how hacking has already, and will continue, to affect the political process.

The following chapter's viewpoints explore the issue of hacking and its effects on the politics of the United States. It also touches on the issue of "hacktivism," where hackers use their skills in the name of civil disobedience or political activism, supposedly for the common good. Hacktivists feel that they are morally justified in their activities, for the good of their country, but others see it as just one more version of what is essentially a criminal activity. Is hacktivism a positive or negative activity? Are sites like WikiLeaks acting in the best interests of the American people, or are they just a different version of the political interference that other countries may be wielding against the US government and its elected officials? These are issues that are going to become increasingly important going forward, in a digital age when so much of the government process and voter information is now digital and vulnerable to hackers.

> "We must implement a series of bipartisan, nationwide, rational and objective discussions about our election processes and technologies so that citizen trust in this most cherished national infrastructure— and feature of American democracy —can be restored."

The 2016 Election Tampering Was an Attack on Democracy

Richard Forno

In the following viewpoint, Richard Forno argues that the 2016 election was not directly hacked, as in votes themselves being tampered with, but that it was compromised by other kinds of digital attacks. Forno believes that this tampering has made it imperative for the US government to upgrade voting systems, and that cybersecurity measures should be used to safeguard the election and voting processes from potential tampering or disabling. He believes that the integrity of the American voting system has been attacked, and the government must take action now to protect this important part of the democratic process. Forno is Senior Lecturer, Cybersecurity & Internet Researcher, University of Maryland, Baltimore County.

As you read, consider the following questions:

1. How was the 2016 election affected by digital attacks?
2. What does the author think the government needs to do to safeguard the election process?
3. How does the 2016 election demonstrate how fragile the electoral process is?

The presidential campaign of 2016 thankfully—and we can only hope officially—ended this evening. As of when this article was posted, there are no reports of widespread cyberattacks or other digital interference against state voting systems. Of course, since votes are still being tallied, we're not in the clear yet. But current indications are that this was a fairly uneventful election, from a cybersecurity perspective at least.

So far, we've seen no public evidence of Russian hackers, 400-pound or otherwise, attacking individual voting machines from their bedrooms (to use a very tired old trope). There have been reports of brief computer problems, but they were easily remedied. And there's no indication that state voter registration databases were compromised by hostile third parties.

Nevertheless, cybersecurity units of several states' National Guard forces were mobilized ahead of the election, in a manner reminiscent of the reassuring and public show of force when airports reopened following 9/11. The military's hackers at U.S. Cyber Command reportedly stood ready to retaliate against cyberattacks on the election—in particular, from Russia as well.

These possibilities and preparations reinforce the need for America to place a greater emphasis on election-related cybersecurity, if not also cybersecurity more generally. Even though nothing suspicious appears to suggest the election was "hacked," we must still make improvements. At stake is the trustworthiness of the electoral systems and processes of the world's leading democracy.

Time for Governments to Act

Politically motivated digital attacks during the latter months of election 2016 raised concerns about the electronic security of the American electoral process. These events included the hacking of the Democratic National Committee and the ongoing WikiLeaks disclosures of email accounts of Clinton advisers. These events increased public interest in cybersecurity beyond the effects of the revelations of NSA contractor Edward Snowden in 2013 and many high-profile data breaches.

In recent months, government agencies and experts (including myself) have recommended improvements to the electronic security of our hodgepodge collection of voting systems.

Among our suggestions are that states ensure their voting systems are modernized, properly updated, tested and secured from both physical and network-based tampering. States must continually ensure the integrity of their voter databases to help minimize the potential for voter fraud. And they must provide a trusted audit trail (for example, paper receipts) for election officials and the public to fall back on. There must be a way to clearly resolve questions about the security and integrity of the system, process or reported results.

All of this requires strong political will for meaningful action. It also means we'll need to ensure the necessary money and expertise are available to make it happen in communities all across the country—admittedly not an easy task during a period of widespread budget constraints.

These concerns align with the basic principles of cybersecurity that apply to any organization. Information resources and their data must remain available and accessible to authorized users, confidential from unauthorized users, and protected from intentional and accidental tampering or modification. In meeting these challenges, organizations must find the resources to implement those safeguards in a proactive, effective, and ongoing fashion.

But there is a crucial difference that makes these particular cybersecurity efforts especially important: Election systems are truly critical foundations for our nation's underlying social and political infrastructure.

Rhetoric Attacked Legitimacy

Although this election does not appear to be "hacked" in the manner that many predicted, I do believe that it was successfully and directly attacked, repeatedly. These attacks did not come in the form of hackers altering vote counts. Rather, the attacks on this election's integrity came from assorted and perhaps nontraditional threats, both foreign and domestic.

Over the past year, Republican Donald Trump repeatedly made vague claims of a "rigged" system, possibly related to unsubstantiated allegations of widespread voter fraud or Russian influence. In addition, politically sensitive information was regularly revealed by groups and organizations believing themselves to be above the rules of law and common sense. And, the media itself became the recurring target of scorn as enablers of the alleged election "rigging."

These claims targeted the public's behavioral and cognitive systems. Consequently, many Americans believe that the voting "system" in America cannot be trusted—even though there is no such thing. Rather, the country's elections operate on a patchwork of local and state rules, procedures and technologies.

To wit: Some states use fully electronic voting while others retain the traditional paper ballot. Polls open and close at different times across the country. Some states may offer a window for early voting while others do not. There is no unified national election "system" that could be attacked or disrupted in a single effort.

Unfortunately, refuting claims of vote-rigging or offering contrary views—even when based on documented evidence—was dismissed by believers as further proof of a "rigged" system.

Oddly, Trump made these "rigging" claims despite the fact that he was the nominee of a party whose own members oversee voting matters in many states. That means his allegations suggested his own party's officials and election procedures were conspiring against him.

All this made it more difficult to discuss legitimate voting security concerns objectively, rationally or meaningfully. When everyone believes their own set of "facts," it is hard to address collective problems.

For these reasons, I believe election 2016 demonstrated the fragility of the American electoral process. It is susceptible to various types of attacks, overt and subtle, technical and nontechnical.

Protecting the Voting System

Efforts to protect the American voting system can learn from the practice of cybersecurity. Cybersecurity professionals work to prevent attacks, and to respond to those that happen, in several ways. They identify threats and vulnerabilities in their systems and networks. They create and execute procedures to operate those systems. And they otherwise work to provide a secure cyberspace for their organizations.

They also share threat information and best practices across companies and government agencies. This is because they recognize that cybersecurity is a shared responsibility and collective efforts are more helpful than working alone.

The electoral equivalent of this problem involves much more than identifying and reducing the technical vulnerabilities with electronic voting machines from their assembly all the way to when they're used on Election Day. We must also ensure the integrity of all election data and systems, from the time a citizen submits their personal information when registering to vote, through casting their ballot, and on into counting the vote, tabulating it, and having it formally recorded by state election officials.

Elections, like cybersecurity, are a shared effort involving many different people and organizations from industry and all levels of government. To carry the metaphor further, let's also take steps to ensure that the proverbial "window of vulnerability" is as small as possible. In the electoral process, reducing the potential time for an attacker to cause mischief is a valuable thing to consider. For example, is there really a need to have a multi-year presidential campaign that can be swayed regularly by any number of hacks in the cyber or cognitive domains?

Errors Still Happen

As of this evening, the process of voting appears to have encountered minimal, if any, cybersecurity-related problems. However, we may not learn about them immediately—unless attackers claim responsibility or government agencies make a public statement. Again, trust in the system, and trust in the people, processes and technologies, is crucial.

Yes, there will be human or procedural errors made in vote-casting and vote-counting. They, like any human process or organizational system, are not totally foolproof or errorproof. We must accept that fact. Will there be voter fraud somewhere? Perhaps. But in widespread numbers? Doubtful. And will votes be changed by overseas hackers? Probably not.

Certainly, there will be periodic and likely very minor errors, glitches, and hiccups in the overall election process—there almost always are. The media will report on them, social media will amplify them, and certain candidates or their supporters might use those reports as evidence of a larger conspiracy and evidence of a system "rigged" against them.

But even if tonight's vote count isn't hacked, the damage is done. We must acknowledge that the integrity of America's election system has been attacked successfully. Accordingly, once people have recovered from election 2016, we must implement a series of bipartisan, nationwide, rational and objective discussions about our election processes and technologies so that citizen trust in this most cherished national infrastructure—and feature of American democracy—can be restored.

> *"The emerging nexus of whistleblower and hactivist organisations should be regarded with caution, but instead of labelling them criminals or terrorists, the security community should study their motives and direct their attention to the fight against organized crime, terrorists and autocrats."*

Hacktivists and Whistleblowers Are an Emerging Hybrid Threat

Jakub Šimek

Many companies and governments have long been concerned with cyberespionage and terrorism coming from other countries. In this viewpoint, Jakub Šimek argues that countries should now also be concerned with the emergence of hacktivists and whistleblowing organizations such as WikiLeaks, which are also cyber threats and are coming from within the country, not from foreign agents. Hacktivists and hybrid actors are just as much of a threat to the government as attackers from other countries, even when their motives may not seem to be malicious. Šimek has a master's degree in international relations from University of Economics in Bratislava and works as a program coordinator the Pontis Foundation.

As you read, consider the following questions:

1. What is the definition of a hybrid threat?
2. What is the organization Anonymous, and what hacktivist acts have they conducted?
3. How should the security community treat digital activism?

Introduction

In the past two years cyber security became a centre of security policy strategies on both sides of Atlantic. We witnessed the use of sophisticated cyber weapons such as Stuxnet and Flame as well as various serious hacking attacks on US military which all had alleged state sponsorship. WikiLeaks continued to publish high profile series of redacted classified materials connected to wars in Afghanistan and Iraq as well as Guantanamo prison and US diplomatic cables. In 2012, WikiLeaks for the first time launched a direct cooperation with the hactivist network Anonymous, and exposed an entire and non-redacted email communication of the private intelligence firm Stratfor. A Similar attack by Anonymous against another private security contractor, HBGarry, occurred in early 2011.

This contribution aims to examine an increasing impact of hactivists and whistleblower organisations on international relations from the soft security perspective. Defence community was for years too preoccupied analysing the possibility of cyber warfare by state-sponsored actors, and didn't dedicate enough attention to mitigating threats stemming from non-state actors with activist or organised crime affiliations. Various hacking operations conducted by Anonymous and its spinoffs, and the unravelling story of WikiLeaks and its founder Julian Assange, are well documented by technology journalists on a daily basis. Instead of enumerating them, this paper will try to analyse this dynamic phenomenon of whistleblower organisations and hacktivist collectives and put it in a larger context of global push for open data in politics and the emerging concept of so-called "big data" and gamification.

The emerging nexus of whistleblower and hactivist organisations should be regarded with caution, but instead of labelling them criminals or terrorists, the security community should study their motives and direct their attention to the fight against organized crime, terrorists and autocrats. In order to better allocate the shrinking defence and security budgets it is necessary to distinguish a few ill-minded and potentially dangerous hackers from e.g. hactivists who played a constructive role in providing technical support for the dissent in the events of Arab Awakening in 2011 and for example tried to challenge the Los Zetas Cartel in Mexico. Therefore the narrative against hactivists should be carefully crafted, in order not to further alienate the young people who support internet freedom and could be at times beneficial to the soft security environment.

Background of the Phenomenon

In the recent Security Jam 2012 organized by SDA with an aim to provide recommendations for the NATO Chicago Summit, a heated debate about so-called hybrid threats took place. During the discussion, Roy Hunstok, from NATO Allied Command Transformation noted that NATO "needs to develop a doctrine for understanding the complex challenges raised by groups such as Al Shabaab, Al Qaeda, hacking groups such as Anonymous or global terrorist networks with no clear command structure" (Dowdall, 2012, p. 39).

The author of this contribution advocated during the Security Jam a need for a different unifying narrative which would treat e.g. terrorists and organized criminals as one joint threat, and thus change the present counterproductive narrative of so-called Culture Clash, where terrorists are disproportionally reflected and other hybrid threats such as transnational organized criminal networks aren't sufficiently challenged. This notion was opposed by some "jammers" who argued that organized crime has economic

WHY WIKILEAKS WORKS

Russia's hacking and leaking is proving a far more potent threat to our democracy than nuclear weapons.

Why launch warheads when you can blow up a political system from inside? That is the message of the latest WikiLeaks "exposé" of CIA hacking tools.

The truth is simple. Intelligence agencies conduct intelligence operations. There is a clue in the name.

Western intelligence agencies spy on our adversaries—Russia, China, Iran, organized crime and other targets. That is what they are paid to do. They recruit agents and also use electronic tricks. They work on their own and in conjunction with allies.

They are rather good at this. It would be surprising—and a real scandal—if they were not.

Neither in the material stolen by the defector Edward Snowden, nor in the latest data heist from the CIA, is there the slightest sign of American, British or allied services doing anything illegal or unethical.

They are not spying to serve U.S. corporate interests. Nor are they targeting Western governments' domestic political opponents.

The CIA collects lists of vulnerabilities in old operating systems. So do other agencies. These do not "bypass" encrypted communications such as Signal, WhatsApp and the like. The real point is that encryption is now ubiquitous, free and convenient. Spy agencies can't crack it. So they have to attack the "end-point" instead.

That means getting into computers, smartphones and other devices...

I was a huge fan of WikiLeaks when it first started. But it has long abandoned the commendable cause of genuine whistle-blowers, who risk their careers or jail to expose corporate or government wrongdoing. WikiLeaks is highly selective. It never publishes leaked material that damages Russia or China. It dumps large amounts of documents all at once, accompanied by sensational, misleading press releases and tweets.

For example, it implies that the CIA could have faked Russian involvement in the hacking of the Democratic National Committee.

That would be illegal, insanely risky and politically inconceivable: The CIA, under a Democratic administration, hacks into a Democratic candidate's campaign and releases damaging emails because the spies knew that Hillary Clinton would lose and wanted to taint Donald Trump's eventual victory? Implausible, even by Hollywood standards.

More plausibly, WikiLeaks—wittingly or unwittingly—is helping Russia's attempt to destroy the American political system by injecting fear, uncertainty and doubt into an already highly polarized and overheated environment.

… Vladimir Putin brilliantly exploits the West's weaknesses. It systematically attacks trust—in the media, in institutions, in politicians, between countries.

Russia's tactics work. But only because we let it.

"Why WikiLeaks Works," by Edward Lucas, StopFake.org, March 16, 2017.

aims whereas terrorists have ideological ones. But also terrorists use organised criminal structures and methods to finance their activities and criminals use terror to intimidate. And criminals often use anti-state ideology to market themselves and both groups have certain characteristics of fearless destructive and inhumane behaviour which has a single purpose to achieve a certain goal without considering individuals they affect. On the contrary, most hacktivists embody a different culture with values focused on freedom of expression, human rights and internet neutrality. Many tend to have leftist views and despise Big Business, privacy violations, overuse of intellectual property and classified materials.

It is a mistake to view current hybrid actors in terms of their respective organisations and some defined structures. Anonymous is more of a brand, a label than an organisation. We tend to think of these organizations as some hierarchical structures with a certain central leadership. It is true that even in these types of loose collectives not everybody is equal. Some people are administrators of the IRCs (internet relay chats). But a 16 year old boy from Hague who was arrested after Anonymous in the Operation Payback targeted financial institutions, such as Visa and Mastercard with Distributed Denial of Service (DDoS) attacks after they refused to service WikiLeaks payments, can be hardly viewed as one of the group's leaders.

The origin of the hactivist phenomenon can be found in the 1984 novel *Neuromancer* by William Gibson, where he writes about groups of young nihilistic terrorists engaged in quick attacks facilitated by the "cyberspace," a term he coined. A decade later he described an organization called the Republic of Desire where internet-savvy users conducted pranks for amusement, and sometimes ideological reasons. Actually during the 1994 Zapatista revolution of EZLN in the Mexican state of Chiapas online activists from around the globe attacked various governments, corporations and the WTO in the act of digital civil disobedience and for the support of the rising anti-globalization movement. Similarly, Anonymous rose to public knowledge around the same time as the Occupy Wall Street movement and the whistleblower site WikiLeaks.

Both WikiLeaks and Anonymous were formed around 2006 but got the global news coverage only in 2010 after WikiLeaks published high profile series of leaks connected to wars in Iraq and Afganistan and later US diplomatic cables and after Anonymous launched various DDoS attacks in WikiLeaks' defence.

Since then, both organisations worked in support of each other, tensions would arise only after Anonymous announcement of its own whistleblowing publisher, Par:AnoIA that was established in March 2012. WikiLeaks attacked the new competition as unreliable and without adequate protection for the sources (Norton, 2012). On the other hand Anonymous considered WikiLeaks as largely defunct due to continuous prosecution of Julian Assange, who was under house arrest in UK on rape allegations in Sweden and fought extradition.

Analysing Anonymous

According to Barrett Brown, the ousted unofficial spokesman of Anonymous, the inner circle of Anonymous has only few dozen members. He sees the collective as a force for good with only

10 percent of members having the goal of just creating pranks on corporations and government and opposing the "the armchair protesting" and moral dimension of activism (Rogers, 2011).

Oxblood Ruffin from the Munich-based Cult of the Dead Cow, one of the oldest hacker organizations that coined the term "hactivism" says: "Hacktivism by our definition has certain rules— if you don't follow those rules then you're often committing a crime." He thinks that "21st-century hackers have a responsibility to safeguard the independence and openness of the Internet" (Luman, 2007).

According to Jeremy Hammond, long-time anti-globalization activist and an arrested member of Anonymous' spinoff LulzSec that went on a 50 day hacking spree in the summer of 2011, "anything a traditional protester can do-from sit-ins, to graffiti, to general civil disobedience-can be done online." Hammond was arrested on 5 March, 2012 in connection with December 2011 hacking of security firm Stratfor after being ousted by a cooperating FBI witness Hector "Sabu" Monsegur.

Anonymous first formed around a popular image-based bulletin board 4chan.org and its first targets of DDoS attacks, leaks and humiliations were for example Scientologists for their aggressive stance against opponents and abusive techniques. That is a shared similarity with a whistleblower publisher WikiLeaks. The main strength of Anonymous is its largely flat, fluid and democratic "structure." It differs from cyber criminals that use botnets of infected zombie computers for attacks as Anonymous supporters voluntarily rent their computers for DDoS attacks by downloading so-called LOIC program that Anonymous developed. Nevertheless, Parmy Olson in her book wrote that contrary to the media reports at the time of the attacks against financial institutions such as PayPal, Mastercard and Visa, the "LOIC volunteers" accounted only for 10% of the firepower and the rest were 2 to 5 botnets rented by 3 hackers whose main aim was to show off their power. That undermines the reputation of the Anons, as a collective with a broad volunteer base and shows a rather different picture where few elite hackers with their large botnets accounted for the success of the most famous DDoS attacks (Olson, 2012).

In 2011 Anonymous focused on supporting the Arab Awakening and provided dissidents in Tunisia and Egypt with means of secure communication and manuals, and helped with organizing protests on Twitter and Facebook, as well as launched various DDoS attacks on Middle East governments.

A notable event was a hack of the security company HBGarry and its subsidiary HBGarry Federal by a group of elite hackers who later formed an Anonymous spinoff called LulzSec. In February 2011, the *Financial Times* made an interview with Aaron Barr, the HBGarry Federal CEO, where he announced his plan to identify Anonymous members at an upcoming security conference. Shortly after, the group stole all emails from HBGarry using a phishing attack and hacked the company's webpage and even Barr's personal Twitter account. HBGarry Federal with other two companies tried to win a business contract for two clients who wished to launch a media campaign against leftist activists and WikiLeaks. But as a result of the Anonymous attack the company went bankrupt.

Some of the thousands of stolen emails were discussing various surveillance technology products that were marketed also to Middle Eastern autocrats and Anonymous later focused on exposing what they dubbed a "cyber-industrial complex" of private intelligence contractors and security companies.

Interestingly, the biggest challenge for Anonymous with its Par:AnoIA project, and WikiLeaks is not acquiring the confidential documents either through whistle-blowers or via hacking. Far more complicated is to analyse those documents and produce some relevant story that could catch the media attention. WikiLeaks relied on its media partners for analysing Iraq and Afganistan war logs and US Diplomatic cables, but the cooperation later deteriorated. Anonymous with its Par:AnoIA, Anonymous Analytics and a project of ex-member Barrett Brown called Panthers Modern rely on the help of volunteers to make sense of the large data dumps. But as of September 2012 Anonymous haven't yet developed a search tool for its HBGarry emails collection. It is far easier to make news with hacking of major government or corporate targets, but analysing the stolen information seems to be almost an impossible challenge for the hacktivist groups. This creates an opportunity for various corporate, criminal and state actors to fill the void and analyse the leaked information. Thus, the idea of citizens effectively opening up their governments remains largely an ideal for now. The various groups of more elite hackers who stemmed from Anonymous in 2011 and continuous infighting in the collective, damaged its image of human rights activists who supported the Arab Awakening.

Characteristics of Anonymous

- More brand than a structure
- Liberal values and anarchistic tendencies—Freedom of speech and internet, anti-war sentiments, fight against privacy violations, big corporations, autocrats, organized crime. A rule not to attack media is observed.
- Use of gamification—game-like elements in their actions and communication
- Strong use of social media like Twitter and communication in IRC chat rooms
- Strength: no leadership and appeal to young people in their teens and twenties
- Weakness: actions of hackers from various fractions beyond activism damage the brand of freedom fighters
- Most of the members are volunteers who support the group through social media and let their computers be part of the LOIC botnet
- Only few dozens of core members who are IRC chat operators have powers to decide on the DDoS attack target and can control the LOIC botnet
- Since 2011 a strong support of Arab Awakening
- Since 2011 infighting and retribution attacks in the group occurred and various fractions were formed

which later damaged the Anonymous reputation of pro-democracy activists

- Most damaging hacks—stolen emails of HBGarry and Stratfor, both security companies Two public faces and unofficial spokesmen Barrett Brown and Gregg Housh left Anonymous in summer 2011 after LulzSec started attacking corporations like Sony without any meaningful cause similar to Arab Awakening. Brown continues with his own project Panthers Modern that tries to bring in volunteers to crowdsource the analysis of data on "cyber-industrial complex" of security companies.
- Members of LulzSec, who went on a 50 day hacking spree in 2011 face charges by FBI
- Since 2011 more than 230 Anonymous-related arrests occurred, many for the voluntary use of their botnet called "LOIC," none in the CEE

Affiliated Spinoffs of Anonymous

- Anonymous Analytics—focused on "short-selling reports" that discover fraud in corporations, so far three reports produced, Chinese food corporation Huabao International went bankrupt in the spring of 2012 as a result (Fish, 2012).
- Par:AnoIA—an attempt similar to previous unsuccessful one time operation OpLeakspin to establish a platform for crowdsourced analysis of leaked information and a competition to WikiLeaks
- LulzSec, AntiSec—teams of hackers with advanced capabilities

The Bigger Picture of Whistle-Blower Publishers

Julian Assange was in his teens in a three member hacking group called International Subversives that would get convicted in Australia for hacking telecom companies, among others also military targets, in the late eighties. They were inspired by crypto-anarchist manifesto by Timothy C. May and a movement that wanted to secure the freedom from the state on the internet by means of encryption (May, 1992). They were penetrating corporate networks just for the enjoyment and as a challenge. His family lived a nomadic life and often moved across Australia. After he was sentenced to pay a hefty fine, he established a small company, securing corporate networks against cyber attacks. He would later continue to pursue similar lifestyle of his activist parents but on a global level. Julian Assange created WikiLeaks in 2006 with the aim to uncover secrets of corrupt regimes and corporations. He first contemplated setting office in Nairobi as Kenya was first country WikiLeaks reported on, publishing a secret report of the vast corruption of Daniel arap Moi's authoritarian regime. Julian Assange was experienced in cryptography and devised a unique way to anonymize his sources. He saw that the report made instant news back in Kenya after it appeared in Western press as Kenyan newspapers were confident to cover what was before considered a public secret (Assange, 2011). Over the years WikiLeaks published secrets on The Church of Scientology, private bank Julius Baer, US military purchases, Battle of Falluja, Guantanamo prison manuals and Malaysian politics.

WikiLeaks received global press coverage in 2010 after he set base in Iceland, a country that begun to champion journalistic freedoms, where he started to focus on US and NATO interventions in Iraq and Afghanistan. His team produced a video from a classified military footage of a helicopter that accidentally killed a group of civilians, including two Reuters reporters they have mistaken for militants. He named the video "Collateral Murder" and wanted it to showcase the cruelty of modern warfare. Thus WikiLeaks made a shift from more-less neutral whistle-blower publisher to an anti-war activist organization. He used to face opposition and threats from lawyers for his previous leaks, but this time he faced the anger of US Administration of Barack Obama. Later he published thousands of leaked military field reports that WikiLeaks named Afghan War Logs and Iraqi War Diaries. These reports depicted the daily lives of soldiers during both wars and brought new revelations that increased the number of civil casualties and showed that US soldiers knew about the rampant abuse of arrested militants by Iraqi forces. The biggest fury of US Administration was caused by the release of secret diplomatic cables, the communication of US Embassies around the world. All three major releases were published in coordination with big Western newspapers that analyzed the leaks for interesting stories that they could follow and redacted the content for sensitive information like the names of dissidents. But later on, the relationship with media partners frayed over various disputes, and at one point WikiLeaks released the whole cache of unredacted cables. The information about corrupted autocrats form the Middle East, that the cables revealed, helped to spark the Arab awakening in Tunisia and Egypt.

All three US related leaks had one alleged source—a young US military analyst Bradley Manning who was later arrested after he contacted a hacker, who he found online as financial contributor of WikiLeaks and therefore he trusted him and consulted with him his actions (Singel, 2009). The hacker tipped him later to FBI. Manning wasn't exposed because of the security flaw on the side of WikiLeaks. But a string of human errors that made the list of WikiLeaks' supporters public and later made Manning trust the hacker, proved that technology alone cannot promise anonymity for whistle-blowers. After the so-called CableGate US Administration was trying to establish a case against Assange, whom they suspected of directly collaborating with his source, Manning. Previously a long-term WikiLeaks member Daniel Domscheit-Berg split with Julian Assange as he disagreed with the high profile leaks and ideologization of WikiLeaks and established his own publisher OpenLeaks. As was previously mentioned, Anonymous attacked financial institutions that refused to process contributions to WikiLeaks after the 2010 releases and later when Assange was sought by Swedish authorities on sexual assault allegations, they attacked also various websites of Swedish government. The DDoS attacks were supported by hackers with 2-5 botnets of tens of thousands of hijacked computers. A voluntary Anonymous' botnet called LOIC wouldn't be effective according to Parmy Olson's recent book (Olson, 2012, p. 120). After the Anonymous actions in support of WikiLeaks around 230 people were arrested since 2011. Majority of attackers came from USA. The second biggest number was from Germany, but interestingly no arrest was made as German authorities have different approach to cyber-policing (Paget, 2011).

Throughout 2011 the support of Anonymous for WikiLeaks intensified, with operation OpLeakspin that was supposed to crowdsource the analysis of published secret files but failed to attract enough contributors. The cooperation culminated with the theft of emails of the security and private intelligence company Stratfor that Anonymous' spinoff LulzSec submitted to WikiLeaks for publishing. The leaked emails didn't bring major revelations, only showed relationships of Stratfor sources to official diplomats and brought evidence of activist profiling. But since HBGarry and Stratfor hacks, Anonymous and other hacker groups like Telecomix with their Blue Cabinet documentation project and Panthers Modern focused on revealing the "cyber-industrial complex" of private security companies. They found out that often those companies market their products also to autocratic governments and thus help to prosecute dissent and sometimes violate sanctions, even if indirectly through e.g. Dubai resellers (Greenberg, 2011).

In the summer 2012 the relationship between Anonymous and WikiLeaks deteriorated as Julian Assange attacked the competitor Par:AnoIA for insufficient whistle-blower protection. Later even WikiLeaks itself became a victim of a DDoS attack.

WikiLeaks with similar outfits like OpenLeaks, Par:AnoIA, privateintelligence.org, and others are part of an on-going effort by more mainstream actors such as NGOs, activists and researchers who promote higher transparency in both public and private sectors. Organizations like Transparency International and Sunlight Foundation champion the notion of Open Government and both civil society and private sector promote the use of open data, which are easily searchable, comparable and provide a source for analysis and visualisations. But activists are lagging behind corporations in the ability to analyze big data sets. Social media such as Facebook and Twitter are essentially Big Data companies and corporations like Google and IBM and have various powerful tools to crunch big volumes of data in real time and make use of them in combination with their robust Business Intelligence tools. Some Anonymous members could have advanced hacking capabilities but they lack the expensive software and seem unable to find enough volunteers to process the leaked data, analyse and visualize them and make news stories in the same quality as traditional media.

Characteristics of WikiLeaks

- Also more brand than a structure, founded and controlled by Julian Assange
- Positions itself as a vanguard investigative publisher, less "corrupt than old media"
- Liberal values: strong anti-secrecy and anti-war sentiments
- Abstract mission of fighting for "truth and justice"
- Was able to create strong media partnerships, but later alienated newspapers such as *Guardian* and *New York Times*
- Strength: anonymization know-how and tools for whistle-blowers
- Weakness: Controlled by a single person—Julian Assange who has a strong personality and currently faces extradition to Sweden on sexual assault allegations

Implications and Recommendations for Security Community

Due to on-going economic crisis, both military and law enforcement budgets are shrinking and young people in the West face an increased risk of unemployment and social unrest. Therefore a narrative for approaching digital activism needs to be carefully crafted without general assumptions and labelling. Phenomena like Anonymous cannot be regarded as uniform structured organizations. They are rather just brands or symbols that provide lowest common denominators for different actors with various motivations. Some supporters might have pure motives of fighting for freedom of speech and supporting dissent in oppressed regimes. Others might use the collective to showcase their hacking skills and pursue illicit goals. People like Barrett Brown, the ousted unofficial ex-spokesman of Anonymous didn't hesitate to face powerful Mexican Los Zetas Cartel and called for an operation that would reveal secrets of its members to illuminate the on-going drug wars. Other hackers used the opportunity of DDoS attacks on financial institutions to showcase the power of their own botnets of hijacked computers.

Therefore a sensitive soft security approach is needed in order not to alienate the majority of activists who pursue democratic values and don't engage in explicit criminal activities. In the United States DDoS attacks are illegal, but other countries view such voluntary protests merely as virtual sit-ins that occupy certain webpage for a limited time and thus draw attention to a particular cause. Modern hactivists equipped with social media prowess and digital skills are able to launch effective "swarming strategies" that engage an adversary on various fronts and from all angles and employ myriad of different actors and tools to achieve the chosen objective. Rand Corporation anticipated and described this process of modern warfare strategies in their 2003 paper called *Swarming & The Future of Conflict* (RAND, 2003). Therefore, NATO should develop its own media doctrine for dealing with future leaks of classified documents and instead of demonizing the whistle-blowers, it should seek a way to acknowledge possible mistakes and minimize the damage through some proactive communication and search for a common ground and principles.

Young hackers should be sensitized to take responsibility for redacting the information that could be dangerous for e.g. dissidents in oppressed regimes or misused by organized crime. A framework of European Council Convention on Cybercrime should be taken into account and cybercrimes should be assessed against the financial damage they caused (RAND, 2012, p. 43).

As mentioned previously, a new united narrative could tone-down the ideological dimension of various adversaries and drum up the organized crime elements of the enemies that fall under the notion of non-state hybrid threats. In this way one doesn't get punished or ostracized for the expression of more radical political thoughts, but only the groups of individuals that engage in organized law breaking and violence would be singled out and punished. NATO should design its own channels for whistle-blowers, who would otherwise fear to expose the misconduct of their superiors and fellow soldiers. The already rampant over-classification hinders investigations and terrorism prevention and should be reduced, not reinforced (Gallagher, 2012). There are 845 thousand people with top secret clearances in the USA alone (Shachtman, 2012). A third of them are private contractors. Therefore it is impossible to prevent future leaks of government secrets with proactive measures. During the recent Security Jam 2012 that produced recommendations for NATO Chicago Summit an idea to recruit "white hat" (defence) hackers was mentioned (Dowdall, 2012, p. 21). Nevertheless, the more data are leaked, the less they mean. Instead, a more sensitive and focused soft security approach is needed as a reactive measure in the post-leak communication. Also a support of education and ICT infrastructure e.g. in Afghanistan can help to increase the soft security and image of the Alliance towards young people.

Social media play an increasing role in our daily lives and the security community needs to clearly define its approach and policies in the new field of SOCMINT in order to balance the privacy concerns with the crime prevention and ensure that private security companies follow the same guidelines (Demos, 2012, p. 56). The similar applies to various security software products and their export to rogue regimes.

Hactivists have their origin in the cyberpunk literature of the 80's and Anonymous may partially resemble the symbolic of postmodern Zapatista revolution of 1994 and draw on the anti-globalisation and recent Occupy movements. Instead of looking at a unified group one should see individuals with various skills, beliefs and motives. A force that has the potential to move towards a direction of a new generation of NGOs and civil society but also can backtrack towards chaos and sometimes childish irresponsible pranks at the expense of governments and corporations.

Resources

Assange, J. (2011). *Julian Assange: The Unauthorized Autobiography*. Edinburgh: Canongate Books.

Demos. (2012). #Inteligence. Eidhoven: Lecturis.

Dowdall, J. (2012). *A Security & Defence Agenda* report. Bussels: Geert Cami.

Fish, I. S. (2012, April 26). Financial (Secret) Services. Retrieved September 8, 2012, from Foreign Policy. http://www.foreignpolicy.com/articles/2012/04/26/financial_secret_services.

Gallagher, S. (2012, July 31). "How FBI technology woes let Fort Hood shooter slip by." Retrieved September 8, 2012, from Technology Lab. http://arstechnica.com/information-technology/2012/07/how-fbi-technology-woes-let-fort-hood-shooter-slip-by/2/.

Greenberg, A. (2011, December 26). "Meet Telecomix, The Hackers Bent On Exposing Those Who Censor And Surveil The Internet." Retrieved September 8, 2012, from *Forbes*. http://www.forbes.com/sites/andygreenberg/2011/12/26/meet-telecomix-the-hackers-bent-on-exposing-those-who-censor-and-surveil-the-internet/.

Luman, S. (2007, July). chicagomag.com. Retrieved September 8, 2012, from http://www.chicagomag.com/Chicago-Magazine/July-2007/The-Hacktivist/index.php?cparticle=2&siarticle=1#artanc.

Norton, Q. (2012, July 13). "Par:AnoIA: Anonymous Launches WikiLeaks-esque Site for Data Dumps." Retrieved September 8, 2012, from *Threat Level*. http://www.wired.com/threatlevel/2012/07/paranoia-anonymous/.

Olson, P. (2012). *We Are Anonymous*. New York: Little, Brown and Company.

Paget, F. (2011, October 21). "The Rise and Fall of Anonymous." Retrieved September 8, 2012, from McAffee Labs. http://blogs.mcafee.com/mcafee-labs/the-rise-and-fall-of-anonymous.

RAND. (2012). *Feasibility Study for a European Cybercrime Centre*. Santa Monica: RAND.

RAND. (2003). *Swarming—The Future of Conflict*. Washington: RAND.

Rogers, T. (2011, March 23). *D Magazine*. Retrieved September 8, 2012, from http://www.dmagazine.com/Home/D_Magazine/2011/April/How_Barrett_Brown_Helped_Overthrow_the_Government_of_Tunisia.aspx?page=2.

Shachtman, N. (2012, August 12). "Trapwire: It's Not the Surveillance, It's the Sleaze." Retrieved September 8, 2012, from *Danger Room*. http://www.wired.com/dangerroom/2012/08/trapwire-strafor-biz/all/.

Singel, R. (2009, February 18). "Wikileaks Forced to Leak Its Own Secret Info—Update." Retrieved September 8, 2012, from *Threat Level*. http://www.wired.com/threatlevel/2009/02/wikileaks-force/.

> "Should we feel any differently when a private party—or a country other than the United States—conducts such a search? To bless it is to condone vigilantism, or intrusion by other states into our own citizens' private affairs."

Hacking Emails Is Not the Same as Whistleblowing

Jonathan Zittrain

Hacking into individual, government, and corporate information has become far too commonplace in today's world. In this viewpoint, Jonathan Zittrain argues that hacking in the name of whistleblowing and activism has made the invasion of privacy, particularly that of people's emails, no longer seem especially important. And if we lose empathy for people whose personal email accounts are hacked, even in the interests of supposed whistleblowing, then we are losing empathy and respect for everyone. After all, anyone, from any political party, can be exposed. Zittrain is the George Bemis Professor of International Law at Harvard Law School and the Harvard Kennedy School of Government, Professor of Computer Science at the Harvard School of Engineering and Applied Sciences, Director of the Harvard Law School Library, and co-founder of the Berkman Klein Center for Internet & Society.

"Mass Hacks of Private Email Aren't Whistleblowing, They Are At Odds With It," by Jonathan Zittrain, Just Security, October 19, 2016. Reprinted by permission.

As you read, consider the following questions:

1. Is it ever justified to hack into personal email accounts in the interests of whistleblowing?
2. What are some of the dangers of hacking into and then releasing huge government documents to the public?
3. How could the lack of empathy on the part of hackers eventually affect society?

The world of 2016 is one where leaking a lot is much easier than leaking a little. And the indiscriminate compromise of people's selfies, ephemeral data, and personal correspondence—what we used to rightly think of as a simple and brutal invasion of privacy—has become the unremarkable chaff surrounding a few worthy instances of potentially genuine whistleblowing. These now-routine *Exxon Valdez* spill-sized leaks, for which anyone can be a target, threaten us as individuals and as a citizenry. They're not at all like the Pentagon Papers or the revelations of Watergate, and they wrongly benefit from the general feeling that such leaks are a way to bring powerful parties to account.

In 1971, Daniel Ellsberg leaked the Pentagon Papers to a few U.S. senators. When it appeared to him that they weren't going to further release them, he then leaked the papers to the *New York Times*. The leak made public the U.S. government's confidential assessment of the ongoing Vietnam War, including its conclusion that it was unwinnable.

> A year later, FBI associate director Mark Felt—a.k.a. Deep Throat—began his contact with *Washington Post* reporters Bob Woodward and Carl Bernstein, helping them break the story of the Nixon White House's attempt to bug the DNC headquarters in the Watergate Hotel, and then to cover it up.

These whistleblowers are often celebrated as ethical people who sought to bring accountability for the government's dissembling or secret wrongdoing. Felt kept his identity secret for years, and the Ford Administration had little incentive to identify the *Washington*

Post's sources as the country sought to heal after Nixon's resignation. Ellsberg, on the other hand, never sought to remain anonymous for what he did. When he turned himself in for prosecution, he said:

> I felt that as an American citizen, as a responsible citizen, I could no longer cooperate in concealing this information from the American public. I did this clearly at my own jeopardy and I am prepared to answer to all the consequences of this decision.

Ellsberg came forward about the Pentagon Papers before the Watergate scandal broke, and the Nixon Administration prosecuted him for having stolen and leaked the documents. But the case against Ellsberg did not begin in earnest until after Watergate, and it ended in a mistrial when it was revealed that members of the same White House burglary team that had tried to wiretap the DNC at the Watergate had also illegally broken into Ellsberg's psychiatrist's office, looking for dirt on Ellsberg in the files there.

Forty years later we have experienced leaks by U.S. Army soldier Chelsea Manning to WikiLeaks, and NSA contractor Edward Snowden to the *Guardian* and other papers, containing tranches of documents so large that neither Manning nor Snowden could be in a position to know exactly what information they were compromising as they did it. Both were promptly identified by the authorities. Manning became known because she had confided her actions to an online acquaintance who turned her in. Snowden was open about what he did after he had flown to Hong Kong, and then Moscow, to avoid arrest.

Fast forward to the fall of 2016. A site called DC Leaks published a cache of former Secretary of State Colin Powell's email—apparently over two years of his Gmail account's inbox and outbox up to this summer. Last week the U.S. government formally placed blame on the Russian government for these leaks and others like it, saying that Russia's motive is to influence the outcome of the U.S. presidential election.

Interesting nuggets from Powell's emails, primarily his disparagement of both Donald Trump and Hillary Clinton, made for a day's headlines in major media around the world. A lot of fluff surrounds those nuggets; an interactive online site by DC Leaks allows everyone in the world to browse Powell's inbox archive as if it were their own, and it includes such trivia as word that his assistant is heading home to get ready for book club. Last week Hillary Clinton campaign chairman John Podesta's Gmail account was compromised, and WikiLeaks has been posting thousands of his emails every few days in a searchable format.

As Steven Levy has observed, this sort of leak is a digital counterpart to what had been sought by the Watergate burglars by bugging the offices of the DNC—occasioned through hacking, rather than breaking and entering. Watergate thus looms not only as an example of a cover-up that was revealed through whistleblowing—the covered-up burglary was itself a roundly-denounced, and criminal, attempt to procure a political rival's private conversations.

So who is the underdog (to many, a sign of whom to cheer for) in today's scenarios? Is it the someone occasioning a digital break-in to get lots of private data, or is it the person targeted by such a break-in?

DC Leaks started anonymously in April of 2016, and it describes itself in a way siding with those breaking in—and invoking the mantle of the powerless against the powerful:

> The project was launched by the American hacktivists who respect and appreciate freedom of speech, human rights and government of the people. We believe that our politicians have forgotten that in a democracy the people are the highest form of political authority so our citizens have the right to participate in governing our nation.

There's a big disconnect between the ideals of this underdog manifesto and DC Leak's actions, though it's easy to simply treat it as a raw news source like any other. A healthy and free press should be concerned with playing into others' agendas. Carefully selected truths can be assembled to make an utterly false mosaic, and to simply publish any concededly-newsworthy tidbits left on a publication's doorstep abdicates the work that many journalists wish to do—painting a true picture of the world.

It is, of course, hard to begrudge the *Free Beacon's* or the *New York Times's* decisions to publish interesting quotes when a former public official's candid thoughts are exposed. If they don't, others will, and there's a strong imperative not to be scooped. And the quotes they've published are surely newsworthy—so much so that the *Times* featured some of the contents of Powell's and Podesta's emails on its front page.

But before we consume the fast food meal of messages containing private citizens' unguarded moments with friends and move on, we should consider the longer term effects on the body politic of partaking too often, and too indiscriminately.

There might be cases in which a hacker's breach of a private citizen's email might reveal something so explosive, so terrible, that some might justify the ethics of the breach—or at least not deem the fruits of the breach off-limits from further coverage. But it's worth noting that the Fourth Amendment's broad prohibition against warrantless searches means that an unwarranted *government* hack of someone's account, revealing terrible wrongdoing, would not only be cause for damages against the government, but exclusion of that evidence in any criminal case brought against the wrongdoer. The "exclusionary rule" was designed precisely for the purpose of vindicating individual rights, drawing a line with few exceptions where the ends cannot justify the means.

Should we feel any differently when a private party—or a country other than the United States—conducts such a search? To bless it is to condone vigilantism, or intrusion by other states into our own citizens' private affairs. Few would welcome a self-designated house intruder who, in the name of "the right to participate in governing our nation," breaks into people's homes, finds their old files, and then publishes them online for others to look through. Whatever that activity is, it's not whistleblowing. In fact, it's antithetical to whatever values might be said to be behind legitimate whistleblowing.

This point is not academic. Recently DC Leaks published apparently-complete personal email troves from a White House "advance associate"—a person responsible for arranging the logistics of visits—so now anyone can check out the updates from his college fraternity and his efforts with his family to lock down plans for his college graduation weekend. This hack and others like it reveal no official wrongdoing; they leak no official government or institutional documents; and they expose private citizens without any recourse, because they're undertaken anonymously.

To crack people's online accounts is a moral wrong, full stop. And apart from the wrong to the people hacked—Colin Powell will surely get over it, though that's less sure of the young advance team member whose personal emails were also compromised—it is a chilling reminder, and signal, that anyone can be similarly exposed. Republican, Democrat, Libertarian, or Green—the message is that if you stick your neck out publicly by expressing a view on social media that others could disagree with, or choosing to work on a campaign, you and those with whom you correspond privately could pay a price.

There are those who think the American political system is so utterly corrupt that embarrassment to anyone taking part in it at any level is a good way to "burn it all down;" to them, discouraging people from participating is a feature, not a bug. But to anyone who sees civic and political participation as the most important way to advance democracy, and to beat back any capture by special interests, this is not medicine. It is poison. And it can be injected from afar—organizations with no identity or affiliation with a state and its polity can from a distance effect the kinds of leaks that before, short of foreign spying with agents on the ground coupled with the rare public leak of what was found, were produced by people who themselves were intertwined with the systems they were challenging.

Still others might look at today's free-for-all and say that whoever dares to use email—a notoriously insecure medium— has it coming. The underlying idea is as if someone were foolish enough to leave the front door of a house open before going on vacation. But the more accurate analogy is daring to have a house at all—with a door using a lock that can be picked. Which is to say, all of them, or at least those without occupants so conscientious—and wealthy—that they can afford special security.

This lack of empathy is corrosive, because over time continued leaks will lead people to keep their thoughts to themselves, or to furtively communicate unpopular views only in person. That's profoundly unhealthy for a society. It calls to mind the Soviet Union or East Germany: environments representing the opposite of respect for human rights. We need the freedom to associate and communicate without constant fear of surveillance, whether from the state or from strangers. And worse, hacking and selective release means that the hackers and anyone they answer to—such as other countries—can intervene in our public discourse, and our elections, in ways that slant public perceptions and views to suit their own motives.

Whatever you think of the columns of Thomas Friedman, or George Will, or Jennifer Rubin, or anyone writing for *RedState* or the *Huffington Post*, it's astounding to contemplate that such writers face the prospect of hacking by, say, Russia, should they say anything contrary to Russia's state interest. That hacking could not only include release of private email and photos, but also entail compromise of online bank accounts, and it could make writers think twice before daring to put certain ideas to paper.

Worse, there's no reason to think that hackers who say they're providing accountability will stick to politics. The tools can and will be deployed against anyone—any slight or grudge will do, no matter how personal. This challenges a notion that hacks against public figures can be ethically separated over the long term from hacks against private ones, just as more and more people move back and forth between the private and public spheres. Celebrities, web personalities, people who happen to accrue large follower counts, sometimes overnight—what would make these legitimate targets? Even if the distinction between private and public figures as targets could be defined, that obscures the fact that each is entitled to privacy for personal correspondence. Public figures who must adopt an official tone at all times will become that much more wooden and detached from the rest of us.

There's enough injustice and wrong around the world and at home that handwringing about the leaked email of public servants or other notables may seem overwrought. But worry about this privacy issue need not diminish worry about, and action taken for, other issues, including government corruption or undue surveillance. The answer to a surveillance state is not to applaud private hacking of individuals, and we shouldn't shape our view of a hack depending on whose side in a political conflict is being disadvantaged. Whether it was Sarah Palin's Yahoo account, Colin Powell's Gmail, or those of people we haven't heard of, the impact on them as people is real and unfortunate. When we lose our empathy for that, we contribute to the unraveling of our public sphere.

> *"The intrusions into key networks of the Democratic Party and into parts of the American voting infrastructure are foreboding. They highlight the possibility of electoral interference via cyber means."*

Even the Perception of Voting Fraud Can Be Difficult to Counteract

Ben Buchanan and Michael Sulmeyer

In the following excerpted viewpoint, Ben Buchanan and Michael Sulmeyer use an old example of attempted electoral fraud to introduce the potential for electoral insecurity that are possible because of hacking. While it shows that there are many ways to interfere with an election, all of which officials must guard against, it also shows that election fraud, even on a small scale, can be difficult to achieve. The authors also discuss possible ways in which hackers can affect the election process. Buchanan is a Postdoctoral Fellow of the Cyber Security Project at Harvard Kennedy School's Belfer Center. Sulmeyer is the project's director.

"Hacking Chads: The Motivations, Threats, and Effects of Electoral Insecurity," by Ben Buchanan and Michael Sulmeyer, President and Fellows of Harvard College, October 2016. Reprinted by permission.

As you read, consider the following questions:

1. What does an example from an Oregon election in 1984 highlight about election manipulation?
2. What are some of the motivations for those who attempt to manipulate elections?
3. What are some of the ways in which hackers could affect elections?

Introduction

In the summer and fall of 1984, the small locale of Wasco County, Oregon, readied itself for the coming election. Candidates campaigned, citizens registered, and officials prepared. A large group of followers of Bhagwan Shree Rajneesh, an Indian spiritual teacher, lived in a commune in the county. They, too, organized for Election Day. Worried that their candidates would not win the county election, they devised a multistep plan. First, they would bring in thousands of individuals from around the country and attempt to register them locally. Second, they would use salmonella to poison the non-Rajneeshee people of Wasco County, thereby forcing these voters to stay home. In September and October 1984, the group spread the bacteria on salad bars in ten restaurants. The germs sickened 751 people in The Dalles, population 12,000, Wasco County's largest town.

The plan failed. The county clerk ruled that those brought in from out of town were not eligible to vote. The poisonings, though significant, killed no one and were not recognized as an attack until later. As November arrived, the Rajneeshees predicted defeat and chose to boycott the election. By the next year, the group had begun to unravel. With mounting internal strife and facing federal investigation, its leaders planned—this time using guns—to assassinate the United States Attorney. That was also unsuccessful, and various Rajneeshee leaders served time in prison for the crimes.[1]

Responding to a Russian Cyberattack

Almost four months after the cybersecurity firm CrowdStrike claimed that two Russian hacker groups were behind the theft of data from computers at the Democratic National Committee and other political organizations, the U.S. government has publicly attributed the attacks to Russia. In a joint statement from the Director of National Intelligence and Department of Homeland Security, the intelligence community declared that it was "confident that the Russian Government directed the recent compromises of emails from US persons and institutions, including from US political organizations."

This is the latest in a growing list of cyberattacks that the United States has attributed to state-supported hackers. Washington accused the PLA of hacking U.S. Steel and others; North Korea of attacking Sony; and seven hackers tied to the Iranian Revolutionary Guard Corps of attacks on U.S. financial institutions and a dam in Rye, New York. Russia has, not surprisingly, denied any responsibility, saying the claims "lack proof" and are an attempt to create "unprecedented anti-Russian hysteria."

The next steps for the Obama administration are unclear. As Henry Farrell notes, the U.S. government will now have to decide if it will provide compelling evidence of Russian culpability. Releasing additional proof will be necessary if the United States wants to build some international legitimacy for whatever retaliatory actions it takes.

A number of analysts have stressed the challenges facing the United States in responding to these attacks, and especially in preventing the confrontation from spinning out of control. While covert cyber operations would be one example of a proportional response—and the United States certainly has the capability to attack Russian networks—it cannot ensure escalation dominance and the ability to end the conflict. Attacks that attempt to undermine Putin's legitimacy by exposing emails or financial records and revealing compromising information might provoke even more widespread threats to U.S. critical infrastructure. Moreover, as former NSA general counsel Rajesh De and former CIA deputy director Michael Morrell note, offensive cyberattacks are counterproductive to the norms of behavior that the United States is trying to establish.

> Great powers are still trying to navigate the bounds of acceptable and proportionate responses when faced with confrontational state-sponsored cyber activity. Washington's response to Moscow's actions will set the bar for future responses and set the example for other countries who could be victim of the same kind of activity. The White House will want to choose its next move carefully.
>
> **"After Attributing a Cyberattack to Russia, the Most Likely Response Is Non Cyber," by Adam Segal, Council on Foreign Relations, October 10, 2016.**

We bring up this old case because it highlights several themes of renewed modern relevance. First, it shows the range of motivation behind election fraud and manipulation; election tampering can derive from geopolitical aims, but also from purely parochial interests. Second, the incident illustrates the unusual methods groups considering such manipulation pursue, and the countermeasures election officials must take to protect the system's integrity against a wide range of threats. Third, it reveals the difficulty in achieving some kinds of electoral manipulation, especially on a large scale. The very small number of even small-scale election fraud cases is further testament to this fact.[2] Nonetheless, the perception of manipulation can be deeply detrimental to the democratic process.

The intrusions into key networks of the Democratic Party and into parts of the American voting infrastructure are foreboding. They highlight the possibility of electoral interference via cyber means. The Obama Administration's statement in October of 2016 that Russia was involved in at least some of these intrusions is deeply significant, and underscores how the digital integrity of elections is a matter of geopolitics as well as computer science. This intersection of technology and international affairs is a complex and vital one. The aim of this paper therefore is to consider, contextualize, and help mitigate the cybersecurity threats to American elections.

We argue that, while a foreign intelligence service is likely the most persistent and capable threat, a range of actors might have reason to try to interfere with the electoral process. Though actually swinging the result of a presidential election is a major challenge, even the appearance or allegations of improprieties are damaging. It is too late to fully mitigate this danger in 2016, but the cybersecurity of future elections should be a paramount concern. The paper's goal is neither to catalogue every possible danger, nor to provide a technical roadmap of solutions. Instead, this paper seeks to frame this issue and elevate it as a topic of importance. The risk simply isn't going away.

[…]

Motivations

Who might seek to manipulate an election, and why? Though this list of possible actors is hardly exhaustive, this section aims to show the multiplicity of conceivable incentives for electoral interference, the variety of potential actors, and the range of levels—local, state, and federal—possibly affected.

Perhaps the most widely discussed possibility is the potential for a foreign state to manipulate an election to advance its broad geopolitical interests. Trade deals, diplomacy, and military affairs all depend in large part on the political leadership of nations. The leaders of one state may wish to influence whom its interlocutors are in another. For this reason, there is a well-documented history, long preceding the use of cyber capabilities, of states interfering with the elections of other states. From 1945 to 2000, the United States and Russia combined to intervene in 117 national-level foreign elections.[3] Sometimes this influence was overt, such as the American support for West Germany Chancellor Konrad Adenauer in 1953, but in many cases it was not. It is therefore entirely plausible, perhaps even likely, that cyber capabilities could play a role in similar modern efforts. For instance, hackers potentially linked to Russia attempted to interfere with Ukraine's 2014 election; the mechanics of that attack will be discussed below.[4]

Too frequently, though, the discussion of actors with the intent to interfere with an election ends here. This is a mistake that ignores other possible actors and their motivations. For example, a terrorist organization might attempt to undermine the legitimacy of an election. Such a group could have a preferred candidate, as demonstrated by the coordinated bombing of the Madrid subway in 2004. Those attacks killed 192 people three days prior to Spain's general election and helped usher in a Prime Minister who withdrew Spanish forces from the Iraq War.[5] A terrorist group also might want to meddle with or undercut the practice of democracy. The group may claim responsibility for the attempt or attempt to remain covert.

At home, a candidate and political party could attempt to rig an election. The incentive here is obvious. The candidate and party is likely to believe that their view on the issues is correct, that the other side would do damage—perhaps irreparably so— in vital areas, and that electoral impropriety in this case serves long-run national interests. There are practical incentives as well. Access to power, funds, and higher offices could also motivate self-interested fraud. It is possible a candidate could undertake such an interference effort on his or her own, without the knowledge of the political party, and vice versa.

If talented and persistent enough, an individual unaffiliated with a campaign might try to hack an election. This individual could be motivated by partisan concerns, by a passionate view on a single issue, by aspirations of notoriety, or even by a desire to demonstrate the insecurity of the electoral process and prompt reform. This individual might have particular expertise in elections, in computer systems, or both. For instance, it is believed that Bruce Ivins, a senior biodefense researcher for the United States government, carried out the 2001 anthrax attacks; one motivation psychologist identified for his behavior is that the attacks "elevate[d] his own significance" and brought greater attention to the importance of biodefense research.[6] A similar desire could prompt an individual to target the electoral system. Indeed, in 2016 the owner of a cybersecurity company was charged with hacking a Florida election system in order to highlight its vulnerabilities.[7]

Lastly, there is possibility of more attacks like those by the Rajneeshees, in which local groups, concerned with parochial interest, try to manipulate an election. This group could interfere with a local election, but have effects that reach further or are perceived to do so, especially if they live in a swing state or swing region.

It is difficult to assess how many significant actors fall into each category. But, in the anticipation or aftermath of electoral irregularities, officials and analysts would do well to remember the broad range of possibilities rather than assume that a foreign government's hand lies behind every turn. Without such a broad view, a careful analysis of competing hypotheses is not possible. Furthermore, the broader range of actors reveals the limits of strategies such as deterrence through cost imposition as a primary means of securing elections; not every actor on the list above will be easily deterred, even by prison or by geopolitical consequences. While deterrence has an important role, particularly in thwarting sophisticated potential adversaries, the overall problem of election security is made more manageable by solid cybersecurity designs that guard against simpler threats from less capable actors.

Threats

Electoral interference can take many forms. The mechanics of carrying out election fraud via cyber means are crucial to understanding which threats are credible and which are not. This section defines the threat of electoral interference as the illegitimate manipulation of voters or votes in an effort to change the outcome of an election or undermine the credibility of the result. Since the focus of this paper is on cyber capabilities, the typology of different threats that follows is limited only to those that directly employ the use of such capabilities. These are usually network intrusions.

General information operations, such as radio, television, and social media efforts, fall outside of the scope of this paper.

Computer scientists divide threats into three categories: those that target the confidentiality of data or systems, those that target their integrity, and those that target their availability. This framework is useful for assessing the potential for manipulation or interference with the American electoral process. It is also useful to distinguish between manipulating voters (causing them to cast a ballot for a preferred candidate) and manipulating votes (causing an actual casted ballot to be discounted or changed). Manipulation of confidentiality, integrity, and availability of various systems and data is useful for both types of operations. This has long been true—the Rajneeshees' poisoning can be thought of as an attempt to limit voters' availability—but cyber operations offer some new and interesting possibilities in scale and impact.

One way in which an actor targeting voters can influence the election is by making public damaging confidential information obtained via network intrusions. Using this tactic, the actor seeks to influence voters into choosing the actor's preferred candidate or otherwise sows discord in the political process. The most prominent example comes from the summer of 2016, in which Russian actors released internal Democratic National Committee documents perceived as unflattering to the party. After the release of this information, Democratic National Committee Chairwoman Debbie Wasserman Schultz resigned, in part due to concerns that the committee had shown a preference during the primary nominating process. The actor or actors, using the pseudonym "Guccifer 2.0," also released additional documents, including the Democratic Party's opposition file on Donald Trump, a large number of internal emails and strategy documents, and private information on donors and party officials.[8]

Without cyber capabilities, this operation would have been much more difficult to complete. The private documents leaked throughout the summer of 2016 were apparently obtained via network intrusions into a variety of Democratic Party systems. By making confidential data public, the hackers may have intended to exert influence on the political process and on the election. Leaking the opposition file and strategy documents may have undercut future Democratic political efforts. The emails forced a distracting shake-up in party headquarters, while the personal details on donors and candidates may have a chilling effect on participation. But all of this includes some amount of speculation. It is too soon to say what many of the practical effects of the leaks are, what the motivation of the hacker or hackers might be, and—most importantly—whether or how voters take the resulting news stories into account. Influencing voters through the release of confidential information is a lengthy and uncertain undertaking.

[…]

The most immediate risk is that a hacker might manipulate a voting machine so that a vote for one candidate counts for someone else. This is an obvious attack on integrity. One method is to access the tabulation function on the machine itself. Sometimes this requires gaining physical access to the device, and there are a wide variety of conceptual attacks of this kind that have been demonstrated by researchers.[9]

[…]

Another risk is that hackers might target the availability of key parts of the voting infrastructure. By making it harder for some people to vote, they could undermine confidence in the election and perhaps influence its outcome. For instance, an effort to slow the voting process in urban centers in Ohio would disproportionately hurt Democrats, while a similar digital attack on conservative rural areas in Pennsylvania would hurt Republicans. Such an attack could target the voting machines themselves, either slowing their operation or rendering them unavailable. In a 2002 primary in Florida, voting machines malfunctioned—for reasons not related to hacking—locking out voters and resulting in hours-long lines.[10]

[…]

Tabulation mechanisms are another possible vector of attack. This category of operation recalls Josef Stalin's famous statement: "I consider it completely unimportant who in the party will vote, or how; but what is extraordinarily important is this—who will count the votes, and how."[11] The risk to tabulation systems has already been demonstrated in other cases. In Ukraine in 2014, attackers deleted key files from the election commission's vote tallying computers just days prior to the election, forcing officials to rely on backups.[12] The compromise was so total that one investigator later said, "Literally, nothing worked."[13] As outlined earlier, at the machine or precinct level, security audits show that variety of compromises can enable attackers to manipulate the tabulation of votes.

Lastly, the distribution of timely and credible election results is a final possible area of weakness. For example, if automated data streams are used to inform news organizations of the outcome, attackers might manipulate these to try to goad the press into reporting things that will later be undercut or withdrawn. Or they might take control of a reporting stream such as an official Twitter account and disseminate false results directly; this occurred in 2013 when hackers caused the Associated Press's Twitter account to report that there had been a bombing in the White House and President Obama had been injured.[14] Similar disinformation efforts could sow discord in the political process and undermine confidence in the election. The 2000 election, which featured news networks calling the key state of Florida for Al Gore before retractions and a bitter recount resulted in the eventual swearing-in of President Bush, might provide inspiration in this regard.

Endnotes

1. For more on the incident, see Judith Miller, Stephen Engelberg, and William Broad, *Germs: Biological Weapons and America's Secret War*, (New York: Simon & Schuster, 2002).

2. A bipartisan report on electoral fraud concluded that successful electoral manipulation was "rare." "The American Voting Experience: Report and Recommendations of the Presidential Commission on Election Administration," Presidential Commission on Election Administration, 2014, 55.

3. Dov H. Levin, "When the Great Power Gets a Vote: The Effects of Great Power Electoral Interventions on Election Results," *International Studies Quarterly* (2016).

4. Mark Clayton, "Ukraine Election Narrowly Avoided 'Wanton Destruction' from Hackers," *Christian Science Monitor*, 17 June 2014.

5. For more on the effects of the attack on the election, see William Rose, Rysia Murphy, and Max Abrahms, "Does Terrorism Ever Work? The 2004 Madrid Train Bombings," *International Security* 32, no. 1 (2007).

6. Gregory Saatho *et al.*, "Report of the Expert Behavioral Analysis Panel," Research Strategies Network, 2011. Scott Shane, "Panel on Anthrax Inquiry Finds Case against Ivins Persuasive," *The New York Times*, 23 March 2011.

7. Dan Goodin, "How a Security Pro's Ill-Advised Hack of a Florida Elections Site Back red," *Ars Technica*, 9 May 2016.

8. For an overview of the case, see Thomas Rid, "All Signs Point to Russia Being Behind DNC Hack," *VICE*, 25 July 2016.

9. For a seminal example, see Tadayoshi Kohno et al., "Analysis of an Electronic Voting System," IEEE Symposium on Security and Privacy (2004). For a broad survey, see Lawrence Norden, "The Machinery of Democracy," Brennan Center for Justice, 2006.

10. "New Florida Voting Machines Malfunction, Cause Delays," *USA Today*, 10 September 2002; Rebecca Mercuri, "Florida Primary 2002: Back to the Future," *Forum on Risks to the Public in Computers and Related Systems*, 22, no. 24 (2002).

11. This quote appears in various forms. The best source appears to be the Russian-language book by Stalin's former secretary. Boris Bazhanov, *Memoirs of the Former Secretary of Stalin* (Moscow: III Tysiacheletie, 2002).

12. Clayton, "Ukraine Election Narrowly Avoided 'Wanton Destruction' from Hackers."

13. Massimo Calabresi, "How Russia Wants to Undermine the U.S. Election," *TIME*, 29 September 2016.

14. Darren Samuelsohn and Hadas Gold, "Media Vulnerable to Election Night Cyber Attack," *Politico*, 19 October.

> *"The CIA possesses the ability to exploit and control any internet-connected device, including mobile phones and 'smart' televisions. These tools, employed by an army of 5,000 CIA hackers, give the agency the means to spy on virtually anyone."*

The United States Has Used Hacking as an Excuse to Subvert Democracy

Andre Damon

In the following viewpoint, Andre Damon argues that all talk about Russia's meddling in the 2016 US presidential election is hysterical and also ironic, since the United States has long engaged in hacking and espionage to advance its own interests. The author conveys disgust at the US government for, he claims, using allegations of Russian hacking to defend its own foreign policy. This is especially rich, he says, because the CIA has been meddling in the business of countries around the world in order to maintain its position top of the world order. Damon is a reporter for World Socialist website.

"The WikiLeaks Revelations and The Crimes of US Imperialism," by Andre Damon, *World Socialist* website, March 9, 2017. Reprinted by permission.

As you read, consider the following questions:

1. How many documents showing that the CIA is engaging in hacking did WikiLeaks publish?
2. Which national leader was US intelligence spying on, according to Edward Snowden's allegations?
3. How does hacking and spying and hacking maintain US imperialism, according to the author?

With increasing frequency, aggressive foreign policy moves by Washington have been palmed off by the media and political establishment as defensive responses to "hacking" and "cyber-espionage" by US imperialism's geopolitical adversaries: Russia and China.

For months, news programs have been dominated by hysterical allegations that Russia "hacked" the Democratic National Committee in order to subvert the 2016 election. As the print and broadcast media were engaged in feverish denunciations of Russia, the US and its NATO allies moved thousands of troops and hundreds of tanks to the Russian border.

Not content to allege interference only in the American election, the US media and its international surrogates have alleged Russian meddling in elections in France, Germany and other far-flung countries. Prior to the current furor over Russian "hacking" of the election, the Obama administration used allegations of "hacking" and "intellectual property theft" to justify the trade sanctions and military escalation against China that accompanied its "pivot to Asia."

Whenever the State Department, the CIA or unnamed "intelligence officials" proclaim another alleged "cyber" provocation by Washington's geopolitical rivals, news anchors breathlessly regurgitate the allegations as fact, accompanying them with potted infographics and footage of masked men in darkened rooms aggressively typing away at computer keyboards.

But the official narrative of a benevolent and well-intentioned US government coming under attack from hordes of Russian and

Chinese hackers, spies and "internet trolls" was upended Tuesday with the publication by WikiLeaks of some 9,000 documents showing the methods used by the Central Intelligence Agency to carry out criminal cyber-espionage, exploitation, hacking and disinformation operations all over the world.

The documents reveal that the CIA possesses the ability to exploit and control any internet-connected device, including mobile phones and "smart" televisions. These tools, employed by an army of 5,000 CIA hackers, give the agency the means to spy on virtually anyone, whether inside or outside the United States, including foreign governments, "friend" and foe alike, as well as international organizations such as the United Nations.

The WikiLeaks documents expose the United States as the world's greatest "rogue state" and "cyber criminal." The monstrous US espionage network, paid for with hundreds of billions in tax dollars, uses diplomatic posts to hide its activities from its "allies," spies on world leaders, organizes kidnappings and assassinations and aims to influence or overturn elections all over the world.

On Tuesday, former CIA director Michael Hayden replied to the revelations by boasting, "But there are people out there that you want us to spy on. You want us to have the ability to actually turn on that listening device inside the TV to learn that person's intentions."

One can only imagine the howls of indignation such statements would evoke in the American press if they were uttered by a former Russian spymaster. In his comments, Hayden barely attempts to cover up the fact that the United States runs a spying and political disruption operation the likes of which Russian President Vladimir Putin or Chinese President Xi Jinping could only dream of.

The WikiLeaks documents show that the United States seeks to cover up its illicit operations by planting false flags indicating that its geopolitical adversaries, including Russia and China, bear responsibility for its crimes.

Cybersecurity expert Robert Graham noted in a blog post, for example, that "one anti-virus researcher has told me that a virus they once suspected came from the Russians or Chinese can now be attributed to the CIA, as it matches the description perfectly to something in the leak."

The revelations have already begun to reverberate around the world. German Foreign Ministry spokesman Sebastian Fischer said Wednesday that Berlin was taking the revelations "very seriously," adding, "issues of this kind emerge again and again." Meanwhile Germany's chief prosecutor has announced an investigation into the contents of the documents, with a spokesperson telling Reuters, "We will initiate an investigation if we see evidence of concrete criminal acts or specific perpetrators…We're looking at it very carefully."

The documents expose the CIA's use of the US consulate in Frankfurt, Germany as a base for its spying and cyber operations throughout Europe, employing a network of intelligence personnel including CIA agents, NSA spies, military secret service personnel and US Department of Homeland Security employees. Many of these operatives were provided with cover identities and diplomatic passports in order to hide their operations from the German and European governments.

Wednesday's rebuke by the German government followed the revelations in 2013 by Edward Snowden that "unknown members of the US intelligence services spied on the mobile phone of Chancellor Angela Merkel," as Germany's top prosecutor put it in 2015.

The US media, true to its function as a propaganda arm of the CIA and other intelligence agencies, immediately sprang into action to minimize the significance of the revelations and to accuse Russia, entirely without substantiation, of having released the documents in an effort to subvert US interests.

NPR quoted favorably the statements of Hayden, who declared, "I can tell you that these tools would not be used against an American," while the *Washington Post* quoted a bevy of security experts who said there is nothing to worry about in the documents. It favorably cited one such "expert," Jan Dawson, who declared,

"For the vast majority of us, this does not apply to us at all…There's no need to worry for any normal law-abiding citizen."

Such absurd statements, made about a security apparatus that was proven by Snowden's revelations to have spied on the private communications of millions of Americans, and then lied about it to the public and Congress, were taken as good coin by the US media.

Just one day after the WikiLeaks revelations, the media spin machine was already busy portraying them as part of a Russian conspiracy against the United States, and indicting WikiLeaks for acting as an agent of foreign powers. "Could Russia have hacked the CIA?" asked NBC's evening news program on Wednesday, while another segment was titled "Could there be a [Russian] mole inside the CIA?"

The types of spying and disruption mechanisms revealed in the documents constitute a key instrument US foreign policy, which works to subvert the democratic rights of people all over the planet in the interest of US imperialism. No methods, whether spying, hacking, blackmail, murder, torture, or, when need be, bombings and invasion, are off the table.

Periodical and Internet Sources Bibliography

The following articles have been selected to supplement the diverse views presented in this chapter.

Jeremy Diamond, "Russian hacking and the 2016 election: What you need to know." *CNN*, December 16, 2016. http://www.cnn.com/2016/12/12/politics/russian-hack-donald-trump-2016-election/index.html.

"Elections and hacking: the new political norm?" *Safeonline*, May 15, 2017. https://www.safeonline.com/elections-and-hacking-the-new-political-norm/.

Richard Forno, "How Vulnerable to Hacking Is the U.S. Election Cyber Infrastructure?" *US News and World* report, August 1, 2016. https://www.usnews.com/news/articles/2016-08-01/how-vulnerable-to-hacking-is-the-us-election-cyber-infrastructure.

Peter Grier and Jack Detsch, "Russian hacking: the real threat lies ahead." *Christian Science Monitor*, May 9, 2017. https://www.csmonitor.com/USA/Politics/2017/0509/Russian-hacking-the-real-threat-lies-ahead.

Eric Lipton, David E. Sanger, and Scott Shane. "The Perfect Weapon: How Russian Cyberpower Invaded the U.S." *New York Times*, December 13, 2016. https://www.nytimes.com/2016/12/13/us/politics/russia-hack-election-dnc.html?_r=0.

John Naughton, "Russian hacking of the US election is the most extreme case of how the internet is changing our politics." *The Guardian*, September 17, 2016. https://www.theguardian.com/commentisfree/2016/sep/18/hacking-scandals-us-election-how-intenet-affects-our-politics.

Allana Petroff, "How Europe's elections could be hacked." *CNN Tech*, January 25, 2017. http://money.cnn.com/2017/01/25/technology/hacking-elections-europe-germany-france/index.html.

Rebecca Shabad, "Report on Russian hacking released by intelligence community." *CBS News*, January 6, 2017. http://www.cbsnews.com/news/report-on-russian-hacking-released-by-intelligence-community/.

Haley Sweetland Edwards and Chris Wilson, "It's Almost Impossible for the Russians to Hack the U.S. Election. Here's Why." *Time Magazine*, September 21, 2016. http://time.com/4500216/election-voting-machines-hackers-security/.

Clint Watts, "Why Russia Wants the U.S. to Believe the Election Was Hacked." *Nova Next*, October 26, 2016. http://www.pbs.org/wgbh/nova/next/tech/election-cybersecurity/.

OPPOSING
VIEWPOINTS®
SERIES

CHAPTER 3

Are Hackers Criminals?

Chapter Preface

Just as opinions vary as to whether or not hacking is a crime, they also vary on the question of whether all hackers are criminals. There are arguments firmly on the side of condemning hackers as criminals, because they invade privacy, facilitate espionage, and often commit fraud and theft. They can cost millions of dollars in monetary damages, and compromise government security. However, there are those who argue that hackers are not all criminals, and that many of them are creative people with a strong ethical sense. They use hacking as a type of political activism or civil disobedience, or utilize their skills to help governments and corporations maintain sufficient security measures by testing their systems.

There are also arguments as to whether hackers who are caught hacking should be treated as criminals in the justice system. Should a young hacker who is testing their skills by accessing the computer files of a large company be treated the same way as a thief or a murderer? Because hacking is a relatively new skill, there do not yet seem to be hard and fast rules for when they should be prosecuted and when they shouldn't be. The criteria for hacking as a crime is still subject to a very broad interpretation. A convicted hacker can be punished with a fine or with a prison sentence, depending on the severity of their crime and whether it is treated as a misdemeanor or a felony.

Hackers are not all good or all bad. They can find vulnerabilities in systems and point them out, and by doing so they improve security. But they might also create tools to infiltrate security systems, and if these tools fall into the wrong hands, they can be extremely damaging. Hacking is basically a skill set that is very valuable to modern society, but as with anything, it can be used both ways. Hackers who use their skills for good are good people, not criminals, and hackers who use their skills in bad ways are bad people and can be considered criminals. The difficult part is in determining the nature and intent of a hacker's activities.

> *"Not all hackers are created equal. The terms 'hacker' and 'cyber criminal' seem to be used interchangeably in online media which is both misleading and reductive."*

All Hackers Are Not Created Equal

Haylee

In the following viewpoint, Haylee maintains that not all hackers are the same, and that the term cybercriminal shouldn't be used as a blanket term for all hackers. The author explains very specifically the different types of hackers, borrowing the industry standard framework of white hats and black hats from old Western movies, to indicate the good guys and the bad guys of the hacking world. The key factors in distinguishing hackers, according to the author, are whether or not hackers have permission to hack, and whether or not they are gaining personally from their activities. Haylee writes for Emsisoft's blog.

As you read, consider the following questions:

1. What is the factor that distinguishes between different types of hackers?
2. How does a "grey hat" hacker differ from those who fall into the black or white categories?
3. How are hacktivists and grey hat hackers alike?

"Are All Hackers Criminals?" by Haylee, *Emsisoft*, September 22, 2016. Retrieved from http://blog.emsisoft.com

Not all hackers are created equal. The terms "hacker" and "cyber criminal" seem to be used interchangeably in online media which is both misleading and reductive. A cybercriminal uses online means to profit from illegal activity regardless of the cost to its many victims. Hacker is a blanket term that doesn't allow for much differentiation between those who hack for good and those who hack for evil. Many hackers hack for profit. But not all hack to profit from online crime.

In the US, western films between the 1920s and 40s contrasted heroes and villains with the use of black hats (villains) and white hats (heroes). This term has been adopted to define classes of hacker. There are essentially four kinds of hackers; black hat, white hat, grey hat and hactivists. The key to distinguishing between them lies with the permission to hack.

Black Hats

Black-hat hackers, or simply "black hats," are the type of hacker that violate computer security for personal gain. Examples of this include stealing credit cards numbers or mining for personal data to be sold to identity thieves. An example of just how lucrative this can be made the headlines recently when a hacker offered over 650,000 patient records for sale on the dark web; a class of different locations online that are hidden from public search engines and regular internet users. The data, stolen from various medical institutions, included names, addresses and social security numbers. The perpetrator will likely make close to USD$800,000.

Black hat hackers are online criminals who hack without permission for illegal financial or personal gain. Some simply hack for revenge or to prove that they can. The term "black hat" is also used in everyday tech language to describe any kind of person or activity that is considered underhanded or somewhat dodgy, such as SEO black hats who drain website traffic and sell it back to the site owner.

Grey Hats

As in life, between black and white there are various shades of grey. A grey-hat hacker falls in the space between a black hat and a white hat. A grey hat doesn't work for their own personal gain or to cause damage, but their actions may technically be illegal. A grey hat hacker does not ask permission to hack. If a flaw is found a grey hat may reveal the flaw to an organisation privately, enabling them to fix it. Sometimes, however, a grey hat may reveal the flaw publicly which is not necessarily malicious but exposes organisations to black hats who can and will exploit the vulnerability.

Hacktivists

Under the same umbrella as grey hats, hacktivists hack systems as a form of political protest. Anonymous, perhaps the most notorious hacktivists blur the lines of good and bad, always hacking without permission but for what they believe is the greater good. Anonymous have gained a lot of exposure for their Robin Hood type takedowns, such as the hacking and shutting down of child porn sites. They took it one step further however when they leaked the names of visitors to these sites.

When Michael Brown was shot by a police officer in Ferguson on August 9, 2014, Anonymous intervened, collecting evidence to expose Brown's killer in the name of justice. However, after collating all the data they had collected, Anonymous came to the incorrect conclusion and released the name of an innocent man.

Another attempt to seek justice saw Anonymous leak details of thousands of Bay Area Rapid Transport (BART) users. The hack was in retaliation for BART shutting down cell service during a protest to stop activists communicating with each other. Many innocent personal users were caught in the crossfire and had their personal information leaked online.

Though their intentions are good, the means of hacktivists are illegal and the outcome often display mixed results. Additionally,

THE LAZY TERM

I'm guilty of far too often using the term *hacker* to describe cyber criminals attempting to conduct illegal actions against my organization. It's an unfair use of the word and it has been inaccurate.

It's been easy to use hacker, it's widely understood by clients and leaders. But it's a lazy approach.

Using the term hacker to describe cyber criminals lumps those who are at their heart explorers, scientists—let's call them the curious innovators—with the malicious individuals and groups who seek to exploit weaknesses in modern technology for personal gain.

During this week's Atlantic Security Conference (or AtlSecCon), Keren Elazari delivered a fantastic keynote, making the point about the tremendous value the hacking community provides to our modern society. They are, in her insightful argument, a key part of the Internet's immune system.

One point where I'm conflicted is around hackivists. I struggle with the idea that in the pursuit of an ideal, that such individuals often break laws and cause unintended harm. Yet, at the same time, I've seen how the work of hacktivist groups such as Anonymous has helped address injustices such as the initial ridiculous handling of Rahteah Parson's sexual assault by authorities in Nova Scotia.

It's a grey point in an otherwise pretty black and white situation.

Those who use their skills to advance the human condition, to ethically notify organizations and companies of problems with their software or technology infrastructure, are not cybercriminals and should be lauded, not defamed.

Those who use technology to gain illicit benefits, often at the expense of others or society at large, are cybercriminals, not hackers.

I know the term "cyber" is often derided by information technology professionals and others. It's been over used in so many ridiculous ways (cyber hacking), yet I feel the terms cyber security and cyber criminal are the most relevant descriptions still.

I say that because I feel terms such as information security and IT security for example, don't accurately reflect the intersection of people, technology and information that combined create a complex interaction and space. Until someone coins a better term, I'm sticking with cyber.

"Hackers Are Not Cyber Criminals & All Cyber Criminals Are Not Hackers," by David Shipley, LinkedIn, April 19, 2015.

the key objective of a hacktivist is to hack without permission to further a political cause.

White Hats

White hats hack with permission in what can be a lucrative industry for the highly skilled. Looking for vulnerabilities in companies, hackers are hired to find bugs and alert developers or companies so that they can be resolved. White hats often work for profit but don't gain from the exploitation of others.

HackerOne is a company founded by two twenty-five year old hackers who discovered a vulnerability in their university's grading system. After the university was alerted, and the boys were paid handsomely, they founded a business based on the idea that companies will play good money to be informed of breach points before black hats do.

Ethical Hackers are certified by a means of an exam involving penetration tests, whereby hackers seen to penetrate networks and computer systems with the purpose of finding and fixing any vulnerable access points they encounter. While unauthorized hacking, black hat hacking, is illegal, testing that is authorised by an organisation is not.

At Emsisoft, we invite ethical white hat hackers to put our software to the test. We're keen to improve our products continuously, as we all know such a thing as perfect code doesn't exist.

Summary

So, as you can see, not all hackers are the same. The key is the permission to hack and the means of receiving any kind of gain from found vulnerabilities.

A grey hat does not ask for permission but has no intention to cause harm or damage though their means may be illegal. A white hat is hired and permitted to do his work. A black hat is not.

> *"Besides critically engaging with technological artifacts the CCC puts a lot of effort into building, supporting and maintaining alternative infrastructures that enable more secure and anonymous ways of communicating outside the realm of data-hungry, profit-oriented assemblages."*

Hacker Organizations Are Contributing to Society

Sebastian Kubitschko

In the following excerpted viewpoint, Sebastian Kubitschko argues that some hacker organizations consider themselves "hacktivists" and work toward what they consider a collective good. Examples of such groups are Anonymous and WikiLeaks. The author focuses on the Chaos Computer Club (CCC), one of the most established global hacker organizations, to show that hackers deconstruct and expose existing technology in an effort to disrupt and counteract media technology infrastructures (MTI) used for surveillance. The author argues that, in the name of privacy, this activity constitutes a valuable contribution to society. Kubitschko is a post-doctoral researcher at the Centre for Media, Communication and Information Research at the University of Bremen.

"The Role of Hackers in Countering Surveillance and Promoting Democracy," by Sebastian Kubitschko, *Media and Communication* 3(2), 77-87. https://www.cogitatiopress.com/mediaandcommunication/article/view/281/281. Licensed under CC-BY 4.0 International.

As you read, consider the following questions:

1. How long has the CCC been around?
2. How does the author define hacking, for the context of his viewpoint?
3. Against which country's government did the CCC file criminal complaints in 2014?

Since the year of its foundation in 1981, the CCC considers itself a nongovernmental, nonpartisan, and voluntary based organization that is involved in framing media technologies and infrastructures as political phenomena relevant to society at large. The hacker organization explicitly conceptualizes MTI as being embedded in complex power dynamics and act accordingly (Kubitschko, 2015a). After a brief identification stage, the collective registered as a nonprofit organization in 1984 and started to promote their political endeavor of advancing more secure communication and information infrastructures more explicitly. In addition, as a registered lobby group, the Club advocates for more transparency in government, communication as a human right, and free access to communication and information infrastructures for everyone. Colin Bennett (2008) has referred to these kinds of actors as privacy advocates that resist the spread of surveillance and in fact explicitly lists the Chaos Computer Club as a privacy advocacy organization. Ever since the late 1990s, the Club has seen an exponential rise of membership that today figures around 5500 members. To explicate the argument that the hacker organization is acting on indispensable structural features of contemporary democratic constellations, this article will focus on the Club's engagement since the early 2000s. Focusing on a specific time frame also allows us to concentrate on an episode when the three abovementioned elements—popular online platforms, locative media and big data—were coming to life ever more prominently.

To start with, the CCC, of course, does what one might primarily expect from a hacker organization: hacking. Yet, it is worth emphasizing that hacking can take many different forms. In the context of the research presented here, hacking is understood as critical, creative, reflective and subversive use of technology that allows creating new meanings. This kind of engagement goes back to the early days of the CCC and has intensified over the past decade. One of the recent example is the CCC's so-called Federal Trojan hack in 2011. By disclosing governmental surveillance software that was used (unconstitutionally) by German police forces, the Club initiated a heated political debate about the entanglements of technological developments and state surveillance in Germany. This was two years before the issue of surveillance gained global currency owing to Snowden's revelations about the US National Security Agency (see Möller & Mollen, 2014). Here it is helpful to note that the notion of "data protection," which is derived from the German Datenschutz, entered the vocabulary of European experts in the 1960s and 1970s at about the same time as the notion of informational or data privacy arose. Germany, in other words, can generally be considered a surveillance aware nation. The notion of *Informationsselbstbestimmung* (informational selfdetermination), for example, has constitutional status in Germany. This example shows that hacktivism, as hackers' political engagement is generally entitled (see Jordan & Taylor, 2004), does indeed include digital direct action (Coleman, 2014). Hacking in the case of the Federal Trojan means acting as a watchdog of governmental agencies by uncovering surveillance tactics and practices. By deconstructing the abstractness of a given technology—surveillance software in this case—the CCC materializes its formerly unrecognized political quality.

Another principal set of hacker practices to counteract surveillance assemblages is the CCC's financial, social and technical support of infrastructural projects that establish alternative information and communication environments. That is to say, the CCC aims to contribute to create (more or less) uncontrolled spaces where the regulation of the state and the interests of corporations cannot intrude. Developing anonymous communication spaces for citizens has been a project deeply embedded in hacker cultures for some time. The reasons and ideologies of so-called cryptowarriors, for example, differ, but they align in the desire and development of tools that might ensure to enhance privacy (see Greenberg, 2012). In practice, this means that besides critically engaging with technological artifacts the CCC puts a lot of effort into building, supporting and maintaining alternative infrastructures that enable more secure and anonymous ways of communicating outside the realm of data-hungry, profit-oriented assemblages. During the 2008 Beijing Olympics, for example, the Club provided a manual and matching tools enabling journalists and other interested users to circumvent online censorship and surveillance by allowing people free access to information and communication. At the time of research, the hacker organization was operating five Tor servers and was running one of the most used XMPP servers in the world. The Onion Router (Tor) is an overlay network that has its roots David Chaum's (1981) notion of mix networks and is best considered a privacy enhancing technology. More concretely, it is a client software that enhances online anonymity by directing internet traffic through a volunteer network of special-purpose servers scattered around the globe. The Extensible Messaging and Presence Protocol (XMPP), formerly known as Jabber, is an open technology that includes applications like instant messaging, multiparty chat, voice and video calls. "The right to privacy includes the right to anonymity. The only way to protect this right is to exercise it" (Garfinkel, 2001, p. 172). The two systems are designed to protect people's anonymity while browsing the internet and to conceal information from unwanted listeners. The design of Tor and XMPP makes it difficult—and potentially even impossible—for governments to seize the content or to eavesdrop on the interactions. It is important to mention that Tor and XMPP might be considered alternative MTIs, but this does not necessarily imply that they are autonomous in an absolute sense, as they still depend on the commercial internet backbone like cables and internet exchange points. At the same time, these are initiatives that constitute serious alternatives to existing profit-driven online services highlighting that cryptography can be a powerful tool for controlling the unwanted spread of personalized information. The Club's aim is to set limits on surveillance assemblages by making anonymous access as the standard mode of operation across the network's architecture.

Tor is amongst others widely used by journalists and human rights activists who feel the need to conceal their identity due to the drastic penalties that their publications might imply in their home country. Similarly, most aspects of whistleblowing today would be unimaginable without anonymizing services. Encryption is an effective way of avoiding feeding surveillance assemblages with data. Some cryptography enthusiasts go as far as arguing that the technology is a silver bullet for achieving universal privacy, solving virtually all of the problems posed by contemporary surveillance assemblages. Tim May explains in his manifesto, which he read at the first cypherpunk founding meeting in 1992 in Silicon Valley, and later posted to the group's electronic mailing list: "Computer technology is on the verge of providing the ability for individuals and groups to communicate and interact with each other in a totally anonymous manner" (May, 1992). According to May, "crypto anarchy" would, among other things, "alter completely the nature of government regulation,…the ability to keep information secret, and will even alter the nature of trust and reputation" (May, 1992). Yet, it is important to note that cryptography does not necessarily protect privacy, but also protects information (Garfinkel, 2001). What cryptography does in the first place is to guarantee the confidentiality of a given transmission, which is why it is widely used in online banking and other confidential transactions today. Nonetheless, when it comes to people's day-to-day communication and interactions across media environments, encryption is far from being a mass phenomenon. It requires the use of specific services and precautions on the side of the users to avoid accidentally disclosing their true identity. So, this article is not trying to argue that cryptography is the single best or only tool to counter surveillance. All the same, creating, supporting and maintaining alternative infrastructures that enable more secure and private communication means to establish conditions under which ideas can be expressed, exchanged and circulated in new ways. The examples of Tor and XMPP also underline the notion that hacking is best conceptualized as critical, creative, reflective and subversive use of technology that allows creating new meanings. In other words, the hacker organization's practices related to technology demonstrate a constructive way of countering surveillance. By doing this, the CCC is part of a global network of activists that enable a large variety of people to act with and through more secure MTI.

To expand on this line of thought, it is also interesting to note that CCC's engagement in relation to encryption and anonymizing services is double-sided. On the one hand, members use alternative technologies and infrastructures for inward-oriented communication. Since many activities—like the abovementioned Federal Trojan hack—need to be coordinated and take place "in secrecy," the Club cannot rely on commercial platforms or other readily accessible services. From this perspective, privacy is fundamental for the Club to practice their political activities. On the other hand, the CCC brings its idea of free and secure communication to life through developing, supporting and maintaining the mentioned alternatives for the larger public. Tor and XMPP enable people to exercise anonymity and to handle data flows about themselves. Surveillance might indeed be "structurally asymmetrical" (Andrejevic & Gates, 2014, p. 192) as it is generally available only to actors with access to and control over data collection, data analysis, and database management. All the same, as the case of the CCC underlines, there are efforts to consciously and purposefully advance the cause of privacy protection. Accordingly, by acting on digital self-determination and the right to informational privacy the hacker organization is codetermining the balance of privacy, security, autonomy and democratic rights. The Club acts on creating what Warren and

Brandeis (1890) called a "right of privacy" and—in many ways echoing the belief of the two Boston lawyers—refuses to believe that privacy has to die for technology to flourish. As a side effect, so to say, the case study presented in this article shows the human face of technology as it explicitly demonstrates that not machines but individual and collective human actors establish and maintain particular technologies. While the overwhelming majority of contemporary media environments is set up to gather, collect and manage big data, the CCC supports, builds, maintains and uses alternative media technologies and infrastructures that are set up to respect privacy and to honor autonomy. The initiatives that Club members originate and encourage are "interstitial spaces within information processing practices" (Cohen, 2012, p. 1931) that provide "breathing room for personal boundary management" (Cohen, 2012, p. 1932) outside the realm of routine surveillance. Acting on surveillance assemblages therefore is based on critical, creative, reflective and subversive engagements with technology that allow creating new meanings.

Taken together what has been outlined so far, the Club's modes of engagement with MTI can be considered largely technical; which is to say that they require a high level of expertise (skills, knowledge and experience) related to technology per se (Kubitschko, 2015b). The hackers' contestation of surveillance assemblages, however, goes beyond "activism gone electronic" (Jordan & Taylor, 2004, p. 1), since CCC members also articulate their expertise related to contemporary MTI to a wide range of audiences, publics and actors. They do so by means of public gatherings, self-mediation, coverage by mainstream media outlets as well as by interacting with institutional politics. Ever since the early 1980s the CCC has organized public gatherings like the annual Chaos Communication Congress, which today attracts more than 6000 visitors. Self-mediation practices include running individual websites and personal blogs, creating radio shows and podcasts, as well as posting their views on popular online platform accounts. At the same time, mainstream media not only increasingly cover the Club's activities but also grant individual members—in particular the organization's spokespersons—access to their outlets. Articulating their expertise across media environments not only gives the CCC a voice that is heard by a large number of people, it also enables the hackers to raise awareness and spread knowledge related to surveillance and other related issues where politics and technology collide. This facet of articulation is particularly important because being able to act on a given issue first of all preconditions that one is aware of the existence and relevance of the issue at hand. Spreading awareness and knowledge, in other words, is a precondition to enable other people's engagement. In addition to interacting with different audiences and publics, the hackers also carry their standpoint to the realm of traditional centers of power through advising senior politicians, legislators and the constitutional court in Germany. At the same time, articulation also includes legal measures. In 2014, together with the International League of Human Rights, the CCC filed criminal complaints against the German Government for its violation of the right to privacy and obstruction of justice by bearing and cooperating with the electronic surveillance of German citizens by foreign secret services. As matters stand, the court proceeding is still taking place. No matter what the actual outcome will be, the complaint raised the public's attention towards governmental surveillance practices. In fact, making their voice heard in the domain of institutionalized politics and gaining recognition of mainstream media outlets are two dynamics that perpetuate each other in interesting ways.

In the case of the CCC, acting on the notion of privacy does not only refer to doing "stuff" with technology but also the ability to actively deal with both the functions and effects of technology. Put in more concrete terms, the Club is counteracting surveillance assemblages through direct digital action—deconstructing existing technology and supporting, building, maintaining and using alternative media technologies and infrastructures—as well as publicly thematizing and problematizing the issue. By merging technically oriented operations and discursive activities, the hacker organization brings forward a twofold strategy: On the one hand, the hackers open up the possibility for people to use privacy enhancing technology, and on the other hand, the CCC spreads awareness and knowledge related to surveillance and privacy. Instead of exclusively relying on cryptography and the science of secret communication, the Club practices a form of activism that acknowledges the relevance of counteracting surveillance assemblages on different layers. Accordingly, in addition to co-creating interstitial spaces for personal boundary management within information and communication landscapes (Cohen, 2012), the hacker organization also takes part in shaping discursive spaces that establish exchanges of knowledge, flows of information and new levels of awareness. Taken together, this demonstrates that the CCC's interventions in the domains of technology can therefore be conceptualized as interventions in social and political domains.

> "Hackers, unlike other criminals, can
> doff one hat and don another."

Hackers Very Often Wear Gray Hats

Roderick S. Graham

In the following viewpoint, Roderick S. Graham argues that answering the question of whether or not hackers are criminals can be more complex than black and white. The author begins by addressing the potentially criminal activity of a previously-classified white hat hacker, and how his allegedly black-hat actions have caused confusion. It is motivation, the author contends, that distinguishes the classifications of hackers, since they all essentially do the same work. But what complicates matters is that the law doesn't care about motivation, only action. It is possible that all hackers are criminals to some extent, and that they switch hats depending on the job. Graham is assistant professor of sociology at Old Dominion University.

As you read, consider the following questions:

1. Why does the experience of "MalwareTech" interest the viewpoint's author?
2. What are the three officially recognized categories of the hacker subculture?
3. What is the crime, regarding the creation of malware, as quoted in this viewpoint?

The arrest of a British cybersecurity researcher on charges of disseminating malware and conspiring to commit computer fraud and abuse provides a window into the complexities of hacking culture.

In May, a person going by the nickname "MalwareTech" gained international fame—and near-universal praise—for figuring out how to slow, and ultimately effectively stop, the worldwide spread of the WannaCry malware attack. But in August, the person behind that nickname, Marcus Hutchins, was arrested on federal charges of writing and distributing a different malware attack first spotted back in 2014.

The judicial system will sort out whether Hutchins, who has denied wrongdoing and pleaded not guilty, will face as much as 40 years in prison. But to me as a sociologist studying the culture and social patterns of cybercrime, Hutchins' experience is emblematic of the values, beliefs and practices of many hackers.

The Hacker Ethic

The term "hacking" has its origins in the 1950s and 1960s at MIT, where it was used as a positive label to describe someone who tinkers with computers. Indeed, the use of the word "hack," signifying a clever or innovative use of something, is derived from this original meaning. Although the term may have originated at MIT, young people interested in computer technology were tinkering across the country. Technology journalist Steven Levy, in his well-regarded history of that period, writes that these early tinkerers were influenced by the countercultural milieu of the 1960s.

They developed a shared subculture, combining a disdain for tradition, a desire for an open society and optimistic views of how technology could transform people's lives. Levy encapsulated this subculture into a series of beliefs he labeled the "hacker ethic."

People who subscribe to the hacker ethic commonly have a disregard for traditional status markers, like class, age or educational credentials. In this sense, hacking is open, democratic and based on ability. This particular belief has come under scrutiny as some scholars have argued that hacker culture discourages women from joining in. However, many hackers have taken nontraditional career paths, including Hutchins, whose computer skills are self-taught.

Another aspect of hacker subculture is interest in tinkering, changing, modifying and making things work differently or better. This has led to a great deal of innovation, including open-source programs being maintained by collections of coders and programmers—for free.

It is also this tinkering that allows hackers to find vulnerabilities in computers and software. It was through tinkering that Hutchins found a way to slow the WannaCry attack.

Different-Colored Hats

Members of the hacker subculture don't all agree on what they should do with those ideas. Typically, they're divided into three categories, with names inspired by the tropes of Western movies.

"Black hat" hackers are the bad guys. They find vulnerabilities in software and networks and exploit them to make money, whether by stealing data or encrypting data and holding the decryption key for ransom. They also create mischief and havoc, defacing websites and taking over Twitter feeds. The person, or people, who did what Hutchins is charged with—writing and distributing the Kronos malware—sought to hijack victims' banking information, break into their accounts and steal their money. That's a clear black hat activity.

"White hat" hackers are the good guys. They often work for technology companies, cybersecurity firms or government agencies, seeking to identify technological flaws and fix them. Some of them also use their skills to catch black hat hackers and shut down their operations, and even identify them so they can face legal repercussions. Hutchins, in his work as a researcher for the Kryptos Logic cybersecurity firm, was a white hat hacker.

A third group occupies a middle ground, that of the "gray hats." They are often freelancers looking to identify exploits and vulnerabilities in systems for a varying range of purposes. Sometimes they may submit their findings to corporate or government programs intended to identify and fix problems; other times the same person may sell a new finding to a criminal.

What separates these three groups is not their actions—all three groups find weaknesses and tell someone else about them— but their motives. This makes hacking distinct from other types of criminal behavior: There are no "white hat" burglars or "gray hat" money launderers.

The importance of motivation is why many people are skeptical of the charges against Hutchins, at least at the moment. To hackers, whether someone is doing something wrong depends on what hat or hats he is wearing.

Is Hacking a Crime?

Prosecutions under the Computer Fraud and Abuse Act are not simple, mainly because the law addresses only actions, not motives. As a result, many things that white hat hackers do, such as public interest research reported in scholarly journals, may be illegal, if prosecutors decide to charge the people involved.

Hutchins' arrest for his alleged association with the Kronos banking Trojan carries the clear suggestion that he's a black hat. The charges say that in 2014 an as-yet-unnamed person allegedly posted a YouTube video showing how the attack worked, and then offered it for sale. Hutchins is linked because he and that other person allegedly updated the malware's code sometime in 2015, after which the other person allegedly sold the malware at least once.

But Hutchins' white hat job is to find vulnerabilities. Just as he tinkered with the WannaCry code—and found the way to slow it down—he could have been tinkering with the Kronos code. And even if he wrote Kronos—which the government alleges but has not yet proven—that's not necessarily illegal: Orin Kerr, a George Washington University professor who studies the law of computer crimes, told the Guardian, "It's not a crime to create malware. It's not a crime to sell malware. It's a crime to sell malware with the intent to further someone else's crime."

Kerr's comments suggest a third explanation—that Hutchins may have been wearing a gray hat, creating malware for a criminal to use. But we're missing two key elements: proof of Hutchins' actions and any understanding of what his motives might have been. It's especially hard to be sure about his motives without knowing the details of any connection between Hutchins and the unnamed individual, nor even that person's identity.

It is too early to know what will happen to Marcus Hutchins. But there are precedents. In 1988, Robert Morris wrote the first worm malware while he was a graduate student at Cornell, and earned the dubious distinction of becoming the first person convicted under the Computer Fraud and Abuse Act. He is now a tenured professor at MIT.

Kevin Mitnick served five years in prison for various types of hacking. He now switches between white and gray hats—he is a security consultant and sells zero-day exploits to the highest bidder. Mustafa Al-Bassam was once a member of the infamous LulzSec hacking group that hacked into the CIA and Sony. After serving a prison sentence, he completed a computer science degree and is now a security adviser. Hackers, unlike other criminals, can doff one hat and don another.

> *"In the USA, the penalties for cybercrime can be more than 20 years' imprisonment, but the definition of hacking is still not clear."*

Penalties for Hacking Should Be Reformed

Sangkyo Oh and Kyungho Lee

In the following viewpoint, Sangkyo Oh and Kyungho Lee argue that hacking is an ambiguous term that is not legally established globally. This has led to confusion and controversy when it comes to penalties. The authors believe that taking punitive measures against hackers will not stop them because their motivations are not in line with classic punishment tactics. According to the authors, the solution in most cases is to educate hackers on the real damage they are doing, and how their work can affect others. Oh is a Ph.D. candidate in radio communications engineering at Korea University, Seoul, Korea. Lee is a graduate student at Korea University, studying Computer Communications and Computer Security and Reliability.

As you read, consider the following questions:

1. How did hacking begin, according to this viewpoint?
2. What is the jail term for a hacking first offense in the United States?
3. Why is a port scan punishable in Korea?

"The Need for Specific Penalties for Hacking in Criminal Law," by Sangkyo Oh and Kyungho Lee, *The Scientific World Journal*, June 16, 2014. https://www.hindawi.com/journals/tswj/2014/736738/ Licensed under CC-BY 3.0.

Introduction

Hacking began as a way to find computer network security vulnerabilities in order to solve these problems and prevent malicious actions. The term "hacking" was used for the first time in the late 1950s in the minutes of a meeting of the Tech Model Railroad Club at the Massachusetts Institute of Technology (MIT). The original meaning of "hack" is just to feel pleasure in the work process itself. However, this meaning was gradually turned into a bad one through its constant association with computer criminals. In other words, some hackers began to profit from the information that was pulled out of someone else's computer by breaking into it. Hackers also spread malicious programs through a computer network in order to destroy data. Some prefer to differentiate hackers—people who do not use a system illegally but expose holes within systems—from crackers—people who destruct systems. In general, however, distinguishing between hackers and crackers is meaningless to criminals.

Recently, Aaron Swartz who was the founder of Reddit and Demand Progress committed suicide. In early 2011, he hacked JSTOR, the paid journal database, using MIT's network. Federal prosecutors charged him with the maximum penalty of $1 million in fines, 35 years in prison, and asset forfeiture.

The Computer Fraud and Abuse Act (CFAA) has been widely abused by prosecutors to hamper security research, to stifle innovation, and to lock people who have caused little or no economic harm away for years. The CFAA was originally intended to cover the offence of hacking in relation to defense and bank computers, but it has been expanded in order to cover every virtual computer on the internet to mete out disproportionate penalties for virtual crimes.

In USA, reforms collectively known as Aaron's Law intended as amendments to the CFAA have been proposed. The major proposed revisions to the CFAA are related to the use of the provisions "exceeds authorized access" and "access without authorization."

Punishment will be administered only if one or more technical or physical measures are intentionally bypassed. Furthermore, in terms of the penalty, the person will be punished only if the information obtained by hacking into a computer is valued over $5000. This change will put the brakes on the CFAA as a severe punishment policy, bring clarity, and reduce legal controversy in court decisions.

According to the legal provisions of South Korea, hacking means an act that unauthorized or authorized people use to abuse their authority to break into an information network by using an information processing device such as a computer. In other words, the current "Promotion of Information and Communications Network Utilization and Information Protection Act" is the same as the CFAA in USA just before its revision. Any person that violates this could be sentenced to less than three years' imprisonment or a fine of 30 million won or less. However, as in the case of Aaron Swartz, it has the potential to lead to an excessive application of legal principles.

As a result, this study analyzes the international justice and punishment for hackers, then compares them with the "Promotion of Information and Communications Network Utilization and Information Protection Act" through specific legislation related to judicial interpretation, and attempts to reduce legal controversy. Subsequently, we propose measures to prevent excessive punishment.

Penalties of Countries

In this study, we deal with the meaning of cybercrime related to provisions of the law and analyze the principles common to the laws and penalties. We will use comparative law methods in a narrow sense. Two or more social systems and legal systems of the country will be compared. In addition, we will perform a comparative analysis of the contents of several laws for legislation or amendments.

Countries are selected by a specific rule based on the data collection possibility unity for analysis and effectiveness. Target countries are the USA, Germany, and China. USA recognizes cybersecurity as the national security dimensions of cybersecurity awareness. In the German legal system cybersecurity legislation has traditionally had the most profound influence on us. Recently, there was a discussion about cybersecurity in China.

We will find the better way forward to amend the Promotion of Information and Communications Network Utilization and Information Protection Act by comparing it to the laws of each country.

Penalties of Germany

Information network for "electronic residential intrusion" penalties in Article 202(a) of the German Penal Code is provided. Information network intrusions method means to access protected information without the permission of the constituent elements or to allow a third party to access to information. The privacy protection provisions have penalty functions, so that no matter what is the information content of the object that has been breached, the act itself will be regarded as a crime. The penalty would not need to be a result of the breaches.

There is no restriction on how the system is used to bypass the security holes, even if access to the information you enter in a position to recognize the crime is established. If a person finds out a system password using trojans and phishing techniques, even if he is the owner of the corporation, it is considered a crime because it was done without the approval of the owner.

Constituent elements of the "access" mean the content of information that can be recognized. Thus, using the login information to access the network does not constitute a crime, so you are not subject to criminal penalties. However, direct access means that the information is recognizable. So, another way to find out the information is not appropriate.

Penalties of the USA

Computer hackers in the USA go to jail for 10 years for a first offence, and a recidivist gets up to 20 years in prison. In addition, any attempt to cause damage to computers will result in serious problems. Even if there is no explicit damage, the attempt to cause damage to computer would be punished by the legislative provisions. The scale of damage is estimated by the sum of the overall damage in one year. In particular, defense or national security cases can be punished without proof.

Causing damage through the use of computer malware, programs, information dissemination, and unauthorized computer intrusion have resulted in legislative provisions being introduced in the federal Criminal Code criminalizing. Distributed denial of service (DDoS) attacks also punished by federal Criminal Code and imposed penalties for cybercrime, such as hacking and viruses. The cybercrime sentencing standard has been tightened. If the cybercrime committed was intentional, it could result in up to 20 years in prison. Moreover, if damage to human life was caused, it could lead to life imprisonment.

The Cyber Security Enhancement legislation in 2002 (Cyber Security Enhancement Act of 2002) has introduced privacy protection, computer crime sentencing detail, and guide for enhanced penalties. Specifically, the guidelines were modified to consider the seriousness of the sentencing under Article 225 of the Computer Fraud and Abuse Act (Computer Fraud and Abuse Act, CFAA). Besides, a cyberattacker who intentionally or inadvertently violates the law and causes serious injury may go to jail for up to 20 years. In addition, intentionally or negligently causing death may be punished by life imprisonment.

Penalties of China

Cybercrimes are not regulated by one single special law in China. Rather, they are covered by a scope of laws and regulations with a comprehensive nature, such as Ordinance for Security Protection of Computer Information System, Criminal Law Articles 285–287,

Decision Regarding the Maintenance of Internet Security, and Provisions on Administrative Punishment concerning the Management of Public Security.

In 2009, the Amendment to the Criminal Law of China (VII), which was deliberated at the 7th meeting of the Standing Committee of the Eleventh National People's Congress, was passed. Subsequently, China added "hacker" to the Criminal Code in order to be able to legally punish hacking. According to Article 285 of the existing criminal law in China, on the violation of state regulation and intrusion of national affairs, defense, construction, science, and technology, the area of unlawful breaching of computer information systems was punishable with less than three years of imprisonment.

However, under the existing laws, law enforcement agencies faced many challenges to be able to arrest "hackers." They illegally intrude into someone else's account, computer system, and steal information such as passwords. There is also large-scale illegal control of another person's computer. Thus, they make a critical impact on network security. To ensure the correction of the insufficient legal grounds, the Criminal Code Amendment (7) Law was passed, while a second clause and third clause were added to Article 285 of the Criminal Code.

In addition, in 2011 the Supreme People's Court prepared for a trial to punish the people who unlawfully breached the network to obtain information or plant malware by "interpretation of the law for computer information criminal case." The Supreme People's Procuratorate pointed out that the illegal market for the buying and selling of materials and tools for hacking was growing and it was regarded as a criminal offence. Previously, this was punishable with only three years in prison. A relatively light punishment was imposed. However, after this trial, it was held that acts such as providing software to hackers are grave criminal offences. Perhaps this "indirect" law is subject to the Criminal Code and it will allow those who commit this offence to be jailed for up to ten years.

Comparison of Criminal Laws

In this case, Republic of Korea court will be able to make a decision according to the "Promotion of Information and Communications Network Utilization and Protection Act." Thus, violators would be punished by either a fine of up to 30 million won or a maximum prison sentence of three years.

In addition, the United States court will be able to make a decision according to the copyright laws. At this time, a sentence of less than three years' imprisonment or a fine of 30 million won or less is applied.

Under German law, criminals are punished under Article 202a of the Criminal Code. They are sent to jail for less than three years. Also, pursuant to Article 109 of the Copyright Act, the punishment becomes less than three years in prison. On the other hand, China court can make an order to stop using it and may request damage compensation.

Punishment after the structuring of German cybersecurity legislation enables the integration of management. In the case of Korea, cybersecurity criminal penalties for infringement of the Information and Communication Network Utilization and Information Protection Act, the Criminal Code, E-Trade Promotion, Information Infrastructure Protection Act, Communications Privacy Act, and other laws and regulations are decentralized. It leads to problems with understanding penalties, and it makes it difficult to evaluate the laws.

In addition, the German cybersecurity legislation on cybersecurity violations and possible penalties are lumped together. Therefore, it is easy to understand the information. This leads to an effective general prevention of cybercrime. Furthermore, in terms of equality of penalties for legal regulations, it seems to be more preferable than distributed case. Laws and regulations are varied; the purpose of each and the operating policies are different. As a result, it is difficult to secure equity through consistency as a legal basis. It will be useful that law enforcement agencies who enforce the law (prosecutors and courts) interpret and apply the law with regard to the penalties in the Criminal Code.

In the case of Germany, the regulations do not disperse. Therefore, it is possible to punish without exception. But, in the case of Korea, there is no provision for punishment. We shall refer to the German legislative system. Penalties for and violations of cybersecurity provisions should be both included in the Criminal Code. This gap should be complementary. In this respect, the German postpunishment cybersecurity legislation is very useful to us. The main direction of the maintenance of the laws and regulations should be on the basic law. Furthermore, the provisions of other laws that are passed are too specialized or simplified, and common details should be defined in the basic laws.

Cybercrime in the USA began in the mid-1980s. The laws on cybercrime were made and developed through the interactions. However, the extent of the actual low level of criminal penalties was, in the 2000s, caused by the awareness of the seriousness of the damage that can arise and the strict punishment that can be imposed for such an offence. USA is constantly expanding the range of penalties depending on the gravity of the crime; however, its stringent sentencing of Aaron Swartz led to unfortunate side effects such as his suicide. This result is a good lesson for us on criminal law.

Case Studies

The Ministry of Information and Communication announced amendments to the "Promotion of Information and Communication Network Utilization and Information Protection Act" as part of its follow-up measures to the "1.25 Internet Security Incident," and to expand the scope of the penalty for cybercrime. Just an attempt at hacking or introduction of a virus can result in a criminal penalty with a maximum sentence of five years in prison or a fine of 50 million won.

Port Scan

A port scan is a subject of punishment in Korea because it is regarded as an attempt to attack. Strictly speaking, a port scan is a vulnerability inspection skill rather than a hacking attack. But sometimes hackers misuse such a skill to find out the host's weak point, and hackers try attacks based on this information.

This kind of hacking is considered a "trial of intrusion" rather than "intrusion." However, it is an action "beyond the limits of authority" allowed and can be admitted as starting to execute an attack. Therefore, it can be punishable under Article 48 of the "Promotion of Information and Communication Network Utilization and Information Protection Act."

But as mentioned earlier, focusing on "intrusion," we can have other constructions of law. "Intrusion" means that the agent does not follow the normal certification procedure for utilizing the resource of information network system or uses an abnormal method to get authorization for entering information network system. When the resources of the information network system can be used arbitrarily, the resulting state is defined as completion of intrusion. Therefore, port scanning by hackers is defined not as the action of intrusion into an information network system but as the action of preparation for attempting to break into a targeted web server. We should regard the installing of a program for intrusion, when security vulnerability is discovered after port scanning, as the onset point of the execution of a hacking.

In addition, just executing a port scan does not damage the system. Actually, one can tell when a port scan is done on purpose by the periodicity or the specific port range of the object of port scanning. The malicious packets are usually filtered through a FW (firewall) or IDS (intrusion detection system).

Collecting Email Addresses

Similarly, there is an act concerning the collection of email addresses. To punish this kind of preliminary act for spam mail sending is unreasonable and prior criminalization because it is unclear whether spam mail sending is a crime that warrants sentencing. We do not criminalize unwanted postal mail or leaflets that are delivered to a receiver in the real world. In this situation, the criminalization of spam mail is an unreasonable action. Moreover, there is no legal provisions to punish the collection of email addresses what is not using some program or technical device.

iPhone Jail Breaking

It belongs to a hack that manipulates the kernel of operating system in hardware such as iPhone for using more than the originally programmed functions. It is a real interesting mix of professionals looking at this. But it is not violating copyright laws. Moreover, it is considered as having no intention to cybercrime. This pseudohacking is ruled out of subject to criminal prosecution.

Attempted DDoS Attack

DDoS attacker is punished by the law regarding the promotion of information and communication network use and protection of information Articles 48 and 71. But this law cannot punish an attempted crime. So DDoS Attacker will not be punished if there are no breakdowns in network. Moreover, the scope of attempted DDoS attack will be expanded by technological development.

Conclusions

Most cyberhackings are perpetrated by hackers to show off or satisfy themselves. Therefore, enhancing punishment is not the best way to prevent hacking. It is more important that they are educated about the damage caused by cyberhacking rather than punishing them. This will fundamentally solve the legal problem of preventing hacking attempts.

As we mentioned above, in the USA, the penalties for cybercrime can be more than 20 years' imprisonment, but the definition of hacking is still not clear. Of course, penalties for hacking are also unclear due to the rapid development of technology. On the other hand, the domestic law for hackers provides a variety of penalties, and it is also not clear. This difference comes from the interpretation. Even if the user simply breaks a contract, unreasonable punishment is likely to be administered. Thus, it is necessary to define rules more clearly and specifically. Taking into consideration the relative uniformity, and the specific provisions of the criminal law in Germany, we must modify the "Promotion of Information and Communications Network Utilization and Information Protection Act" and other regulations. By doing this, legal controversy and excessive punishment will be reduced.

Additionally, reasonable adjustment of statutory punishment is needed in the future. At present, statutory punishment is distinguished from sentencing in current Korean court. Sentencing level converged on the lowest limit of statutory punishment.

> *"Much like gamification is the application of game design principles to non-game uses, the principles of hacking can be applied to non-hacking uses."*

Civic Hacking Is Key for Contemporary Creativity

Tanya Snook

In the following viewpoint, Tanya Snook argues that hacking is a mindset that we all should embrace. The author describes examples of "hacks" in our culture, from MIT's famed pranks to Silicon Valley's approach to design, and contends that core values drive the clever, ethical, enjoyable, excellence-seeking behavior of a civic-oriented hacker's mindset. In an effort to make the case for everyday hacking, Snook provides five principles that can be used to rethink situations, re-evaluate problems, and hack everything. Rethinking our definition of hacking might help us embrace the concept as well. Snook is senior project officer, information management, with the Treasury Board of Canada Secretariat.

"Hacking Is a Mindset, Not a Skillset: Why Civic Hacking Is Key For Contemporary Creativity," by Tanya Snook, *London School of Economics*, January 16, 2014. http://blogs. lse.ac.uk/impactofsocialsciences/2014/01/16/hacking-is-a-mindset-not-a-skillset/.

As you read, consider the following questions:

1. According to the author, what is the definition of hacking?
2. What is the "hacker mindset?"
3. What are some ways that hacking skills could be applied to everyday life?

When I say "hacker" what images come to mind? Some pimply-faced kid in a dark basement, breaking into a high security website to post a picture of a LOL cat? Or a hoodied twenty something male typing furiously with his Guy Fawkes mask beside him, liberating corporate, government or military documents in the name of Anonymous? Using AutoCad software of course, as the movies would have us believe.

But how many of you have referred to yourselves as a hacker? You probably should. My goal is to either convince you that you've been hacking all along or that you really should be hacking. But why hacking? Much like gamification is the application of game design principles to non-game uses, the principles of hacking can be applied to non-hacking uses. And I don't mean by sitting at a computer every day; I mean by hacking in the true sense of the word.

You see, originally, hacking had nothing to do with computer programming: In fact, "hack" was originally a term used to describe pranks performed by MIT students—their pranks are projects or products that are completed to some end, but that also afford the participants some enjoyment by the mere fact of participating. The MIT hackers describe what we call "hacking" as "cracking." When the MIT hackers hack, their goal is to devise "a clever, benign, and 'ethical' prank or practical joke, which is both challenging for the perpetrators and amusing to the MIT community."

The website (there's always a website) dedicated to cataloguing the pranks is actually called the Hack Gallery (hacks.mit.edu). The list of hacks includes lining a hall with invading green army men, installing a lunar module on top of the Great Dome, setting up a giant statue of Athena on a main lawn, and my personal fave, hanging mannequins on high wires and trapezes from a ceiling along with long flowing ribbons, to turn a lobby into a circus.

Along these lines, I found a fantastic quote in the Wikipedia definition of "hacker:" "Hacking entails some form of excellence, for example exploring the limits of what is possible, thereby doing something exciting and meaningful. Activities of playful cleverness can be said to have 'hack value.'" Hack value. What have you done today that can be said to have "Hack Value"?

Now within the mainstream, the term hacking has been appropriated to describe people who hold these same values and do computer programming. But the principles of creativity and cleverness are still there, although the fun may be more intrinsic than obvious to us the outside observer.

It's what Silicon Valley is built on. A recent Harvard Business Review blog post described Silicon Valley as having a culture that believes "things are hack-able—that the way we've designed various systems is not pre-ordained or immutable. We can tinker, re-design, and play with them." It went on to say that participants in Silicon Valley companies "don't ask for permission to do what they do… They are less interested in technologies per se than in playing with established ways of doing things and conventional ways of thinking, creating, learning, and being."

They've adopted a hacking mindset. They translate this clever, ethical, enjoyable, excellence-seeking behaviour to their everyday lives. See? Hacking is a mindset, not a skillset. When you seek, in your everyday life, to deliberately find opportunities to be clever, ethical, to enjoy what you are doing, to seek excellence, then you're hacking. Now the key here is that this behaviour is deliberate. Not a happy accident. If you aren't acting this way deliberately, then we need to change your thinking and behaviour a little bit in order to make this your default MO. In fact, your mission for tomorrow should be: "Do something that has hack value."

I recently wrote about the science of behaviour change in a post on New Year's resolutions. Behavioural science has indicated that in order to effect behaviour change, you need to break things down into small tasks. Successfully completing tiny tasks is a necessary step in making new behaviours stick. With that in mind (and I've probably oversimplified things), I've boiled hacking down to 5 principles that you can keep in mind, and incorporate into your day to day thinking.

The Principles of The Hacking Mindset (according to spydergrrl)

Yeah, these should probably always have the "according to spydergrrl" qualifier since I'm sure that there would be many people (hackers and crackers alike) with their own opinions, happy to jump on the Interwebs and tell me I am wrong:

1. Challenge accepted! (Barriers are welcomed)

This is part of the "clever" component to hacking: accepting barriers as sources of motivation in their own right, motivating you to find a solution to break through them; the feeling of accomplishment at the end being its own reward.

Take for example the origins of crowdfunding, especially through sites like Quirky, Kickstarter, Indiegogo. A lot of the projects funded through these sites wouldn't necessarily get backing by venture capitalists or even banks in order to become a reality. Going directly to consumers to get what essentially amounts to pre-purchases of products and services is a fantastic way to hack the economic system and traditional business models.

In 2002, one of the founders of Indiegogo co-produced a play. It was popular with audiences but not exactly self-funding so they decided to look at other ways to raise investment capital. Indiegogo was born and launched at Sundance in 2008, initially geared to raising money to fund films. It's evolved over the past 5 years to support all sorts of projects: even local communications company MediaStyle is using it to crowdsource funding for a new collaborative event space in their building.

Kickstarter is a bit different because people don't "invest" in Kickstarter projects to make money. They "back" projects in exchange for a tangible good or experience. One example is local tech company teknision who used it to fund and launch their Chameleon app for Android.

Now let's think about you and a barrier you might face at work. At some point in your career (or maybe your whole career) you've likely been told that there are no or very little funds for training. And let's assume that you don't have the wallet to fund your own training. So how do you creatively make up your own training? Thankfully there are plenty of other people who believe in the freedom of information which means you can access free webinars, online articles, and library books. You can find or build a network of people who have the skills you need: joining meetups, social networking, etc. And as you learn, you can find speaking opportunities to test your ideas and your learning.

That's one way. But you could also jump right into projects that will stretch your skills and knowledge: At work, advocate for projects you think are important and if you don't get approval, do them anyway! Partner with people in your network to grow your skills, get experience in a new field. Can't do what you want at work/in your job? Find a way to collaborate with other communities of interest in your organization. Or find a pro bono project that will let you do what you love. I've done some pro bono in the past because I have a skillset that wasn't being tapped into at my job. So, through a friend I got referred to work with a local charity to donate my time and keep those skills up to date. When you find opportunities like this to hone or maintain your skills, you can put it on your resume. And then, hacking your training could even lead you to hacking your career.

Phew. This hacking stuff is a lot of work. Ok, let's step back and start a little smaller.

You get home from work, (stay with me), you get home from work, look up the recipe you want to make tonight and notice you have all the wrong ingredients. But if you throw away the recipe and modify your expectations to make something with what you had, you'll realize that you had all the right ingredients all along. Just the wrong recipe.

Those are the small tasks I was talking about; tiny wins that can help you make hacking your default behaviour. A barrier might only exist due to a perception issue: do you have the wrong tools or do you have the right tools but are looking at the problem from a particular perspective which is limiting your ability to think beyond it? Which brings me to my next principle…

2. Blow away the box. Look for unexpected ways to make something better.

You've probably heard the adage: if you have a hammer, everything looks like a nail. Need proof? Watch a kid walk around the house with a toy hammer. You know it's true. The problem as adults is that we become too practical and start to limit our thinking: only nails look like nails. Sometimes, finding the fun or creative way to approach to something, means that we need to step back to the place where everything looked like a nail.

Take social media, for example. If you've ever had to explain to someone that Twitter is not millions of people posting their lunch, and that there is a lot to gain from investing a little bit of time each day in reading blogs or answering questions on Quora, then you know exactly what I am talking about. Those people think nails are nails: networking happens at formal corporate events, training takes place in boardrooms and classrooms, and it is necessary to respect the hierarchical chain of command. Riiight.

But you know that everything is a nail. You know that you will find out much more in 5 minutes on Twitter first thing in the morning than by spending an hour reading one newspaper or magazine. You have figured out how to get value, how to find what you need out of a noisy, messy system where others only see chaos. Which is why you follow hundreds if not thousands of thought leaders on Twitter. You've chatted with them in the comments section of their blogs. You've rubbed elbows with them (or *gasp* senior executives) at informal, non-work-related networking events (aka meetups).

Maybe you've offered yourself up as a reverse mentor to share your knowledge with your senior executives. Don't have a reverse mentoring program at work? The basic idea is that working level, even entry level, employees mentor the executives in a subject area that execs are less exposed to. It could be anything: social media, user experience, web development, new classification trends. In turn, it gives staff the opportunity for some face time with those they might not see very often. Win-win. If you have a reverse mentoring program, get in on it. If you don't, start one. Chances are, you'll probably skip a couple of rungs on your way up the ladder, yourself.

See, you're already hacking.

Now, going beyond thinking outside the box, and actually blowing away the box can be difficult because it requires you to know who you are. That means not defining yourself by how others define you. Take for instance Ada Lovelace. She was the first reknown woman mathematician and computing specialist, back in the 1800s, when men were men and women were at home.

You're not just a "fill-in-the-blank-with-your-title-here," you're a mentor, a teacher, a coach, an advisor... Hacking your approach and blowing away the box means not allowing your thinking to be limited by the rules and restrictions that others put up around you. It means being confident enough to take a risk, and trusting your gut especially when it seems to have more conviction than your mind.

For example, maybe your library looks like a library but deep down it's actually a seed bank or a planetarium or even an open source community centre. Let's start with the seed bank. Basalt, Colorado has a public library that has started a seed bank. Not just to catalogue and store the seeds, but to enable citizens to check out seeds and plant them at home! In exchange, the borrowers take the best produce from their crops, harvest the seeds and return them to the library for someone else to use. The seed bank is expected to evolve since some crops will succeed and others will fail, the strongest always coming back into the bank. Over time, it could evolve to serve as an effective, proven index of the vegetation that is best suited to the climate and soil in that region.

If all libraries opened up seed banks, they could catalogue and store all of the best crops for each region of the country, an extremely valuable inventory in times of drought or other natural disaster. Not to mention, since librarians are masters of classification and information management, you just know those seeds would be classified and organized like nobody's business. It's a match made in info-science heaven.

For the most part, blowing away the box may mean changing your perception, taking risks and testing out assumptions out on a limb. But if you have built a strong, supportive network and if you have crowdsourced your ideas, then chances are you won't be alone when it's time to challenge traditional approaches. And that's another great thing about hacking: hackers have each other's back.

3. Bring your friends. Unique perspectives create more robust solutions.

A colleague of mine recently tweeted that "we cannot solve a complex problem with a solution from a single discipline of study #justsaying"—Ralph Mercer (@ralphmercer) December 4, 2012. Which is one of the reasons why I love hackfests. Now, I don't consider myself a coder. I think of my abilities in HTML, JavaScript and CSS as coding-light. So when someone suggested I attend a hackfest, I thought that was probably one of the most intimidating ideas ever.

And then I worked as a business analyst in R&D, collaborating with technical architects and developers, whiteboarding solutions and brainstorming development approaches. And I realized that going to a hackfest would be no different. As I wrote late last year about LearnHack YOW, hosted by OpenData Ottawa, it takes all kinds to come up with a solution. You need experienced developers, analysts, user experience types and especially users. Non-hackers are as important to a good hackfest as hackers are... how else will you know if your solution will be useful and usable outside of the hackfest bubble?

Now think about your local library. What if it was an open source loving, hackfest hosting community centre? Maybe it has a ton of computers that were once used for looking up physical copies of books, but with e-readers and digital media taking over, they lie dormant most days. So what it they were offered up as web terminals for hackfests. The library could line up extra sets of tables and chairs where hackers and non-hackers can come together to talk about their open data needs and brainstorm app ideas using the City's data. Your data. Maybe they could even host hackathons for Little Geeks, encouraging them to think about data and how it can improve not only their lives but that of those around them. Maybe our libraries rekindle their role as the heart of the community; a gathering place for people and the birthplace for new ideas.

Even the MIT hackers understood the importance of being a part of something bigger than yourself. It's why people join social groups, volunteer, even play massively multiplayer online role playing games like World of Warcraft or Halo. It's even why people play Farmville and tend to each other's crops.

Outside of the development space, there are plenty of examples of collaborative solution building, or as we now refer to it: crowdsourcing. The first time I came across it was back in the mid-2000s with the Dell Social Innovation Challenge. This was a contest open to post-secondary students across the entire globe, in which they submitted ideas for social change. They posted them to an interactive site, and the general public could vote them up or down. The prize was a scholarship, and the potential to work on their idea.

More recently, there was the public consultation on the Icelandic constitution. If you didn't check it out, it was posted on a wiki, so anyone could log in and make changes. All of the changes were recorded in the history, so it was possible to sift through the evolution of the document over time (and revert to a previous version if it got vandalized).

And you? If you need to work through a question or an idea, if you need to whiteboard an issue, who do you turn to? Have you built up a network of resources that you can tap when you need help? Maybe you have, and you call on subject matter experts for help with work, with technical knowledge. But what about calling on someone who has absolutely nothing to do with the project/department? No experience or subject matter expertise at all? Would you ask your mom for help on a work issue? Probably not.

Maybe your question seems technical but actually has an interpersonal angle you just aren't noticing. Maybe your personality conflict has an underlying technical issue. In the same way that a hackfest needs to be multidisciplinary and reach across all sorts of stakeholder groups to be the most effective, maybe you should reconsider your network and include people who can bring in completely new perspectives, and are more than happy to share their knowledge to help you evolve your thinking. Which brings me to point #4...

4. Give it away now. Information and knowledge should be shared openly, freely.

Sharing information empowers others to change the world. Well, at least their part of the world. Now I may have a bit more of an extreme view of these things than the average person, but I believe that information deserves to be free; research, knowledge, history, these are all beneficial to all of us. And hoarding them or locking them down in the name of intellectual property or profit is counter-intuitive to innovation.

Now you might not be able to decide what to do with the information or data that you work with if you're employed by someone else, so how can you infuse this giving nature into your own life? By giving away your knowledge: post it, assign a creative commons license, do pro bono work, make it open source, give away your expertise.

If you've never used a creative commons license, it's like a copyright on intellectual property that allows others to build on your content as long as they reference you. There are several tiers of licenses that can apply to any IP such as images, content, and media. There are even sites like ccMixter where people will post music for re-use (you will often hear CBC mention creative commons music credits). You might have even used Wikimedia Commons (with full attribution, of course), which is a site where people will share their media for re-use.

But you can also license your own content on your own site. For example, when I post my presentations, I do so with a Creative Commons attribution. I post my full scripts and slides, and open them up so that anyone else can re-use or riff on them at their leisure, as long as they credit me for the original content.

You can also look at community activities that foster information sharing, some easier than others: I mentioned pro bono but you might also consider a for-donation project, where you donate the proceeds. One that you might have heard of (or even been part of) is the 100 Strangers Project by Kim Usan. She took photos of 100 strangers over the course of a year, blogged their stories and then did an art show and sold a coffee table book. All the proceeds went to a charity that was near and dear to her heart.

Closer to home, and more manageable on a day-to-day basis, you can contribute to open information, open source and open data projects. You could also be contributing to community-knowledge wikis like wikipedia or those for makers or even Lego lovers. Or contributing information or classification to all sorts of collaborative projects. Don't know where to start? Check out Code4Lib, which is a collaboration of coders for libraries and libraries for coders working to evolve libraries and library tech. Now, that said, you don't need to be technical to contribute (you should know by now that it doesn't take a developer to hack) and the best part is that they share their projects openly for re-use.

There are also some really fantastic and surprising open source projects. Like Stellarium, an open source planetarium app. It's maintained by the development community and can run off a simple desktop, allowing users to pan and zoom skies all over the world. If you're an astronomy buff or are multilingual, they need your help developing new catalogues and translating their content. Oh, and the app is free and openly available for use. Imagine dedicating a space in our school libraries to showcase the skies, with computers that allow visitors to test drive the heavens for themselves. Did I mention that it's free? And it's actively maintained and it contains more than 600,000 star catalogs. Bet we don't have anything like that on our library shelves right now. If it's good enough for planetarium projection systems, it must be good enough for our schools.

Need more ideas on sharing your knowledge? You could openly blog on your areas of expertise, organize a community learning event or unconference, teach a class. You could even donate some time to your kid's school to teach them something in your area of expertise because we need to…

5. Pay it forward. Teach the next generation to think like a hacker.

Hubby and I are raising a hacker. The running joke in our house is that The Dude will get arrested for hacking into some website when he's 17 and he'll tell the police that his mom taught him how to hack. But that's not the type of hacking we're teaching him. We're teaching him to hack his thinking, to think like a hacker to solve problems.

The whole idea of teaching him to hack actually started last Christmas. I found a set of instructions to build a Star Wars Lego DeathStar tree ornament. Hubby and the Dude took a look at the instructions and decided that they didn't have the right pieces to build it. We have 10,000 pieces of Lego. And this ornament used about 100. So, I got a bit frustrated when I heard this. They were really limiting their thinking.

So I asked the Dude if he knew what hacking was, and told him that we were going to hack the Lego. I made him think up all sorts of combinations to substitute the pieces we didn't have. I made him figure out how we could rework the instructions to suit the pieces we could find in his Lego bin. He was so proud when we finished building it. He even started to refer to himself as a hacker. These days, he knows exactly what I mean when he brings me a problem and I tell him to "hack it." He knows that means to look at the problem again and to reimagine the solution in a new way.

Kids have the most unique perspectives; their thinking is not limited as is ours, they are very perceptive. Some of their ideas are crazy but given a real problem, they will often come up with very real solutions. The Dude begged me to bring him to a hackfest a couple of months ago and it was one of the most fun activities we've done together.

I explained all of the data sets to him in simple terms and had him design his own app concept on paper. He didn't draw it, but wrote down the functions and features that it would have. It might have been easier for him to just draw a picture but by making him think about the functionality, he had to spend a little more time thinking from the user's perspective and understanding what they would want out of it. And it got me thinking about hackfests in schools. It would be so easy to bring a simple hackfest into the classroom and have kids make up their own apps. Any time it's possible to demonstrate the real-life applicability of their studies, kids seem to get more engaged in their learning.

But teaching a hacker, fostering hacking in the next generation doesn't have to be so formal. It can start small with game or toy hacking, in our case, Lego hacking. We'll often check out Brickipedia (yes, a Lego wiki!) for ideas and instructions for sets we don't own. We make him Google ideas, science experiments and definitions when he has questions. We try to turn his questions into opportunities for problem solving and hacking.

And this. If some of you read today's post, you'll know what this is. It's the walker of a 4 year old who recently had surgery on both legs. He hated his walker and didn't want to use it for therapy because he associated it with pain. A friend of his mom's commented that the shape reminded her of an At-At walker. So a friend of the family, who happens to be a cartoonist, hacked it and turned it into an At-At walker. Needless to say, the kid loves his walker now and especially walking around the house pew-pewing his family. A little hacking goes a long way.

It's important to teach kids to hack and actually call it that; to explain to them the importance of reinventing problems, working around constraints, and modding whatever they've been given. At home, at school, when our kids says something is impossible, make it a priority to prove them wrong. These are skills that can serve them their entire lives. And it starts with us modeling the behaviour, and hacking ourselves.

There you go. The Principles of The Hacking Mindset (according to spydergrrl):

1. Challenge accepted! (Barriers are welcomed)
2. Blow away the box. Look for unexpected ways to make something better.
3. Bring your friends. Unique perspectives create more robust solutions.
4. Give it away now. Information and knowledge should be shared openly, freely.
5. Pay it forward. Teach the next generation to think like a hacker.

Based on the original definition of hacking, these are 5 principles that you can use to rethink situations, re-evaluate problems, and hack everything you do. So, if hacking is the application of hacking principles to everyday life, then I'll ask again, how many of you would be willing to call yourselves hackers after you leave here today?

Periodical and Internet Sources Bibliography

The following articles have been selected to supplement the diverse views presented in this chapter.

Christopher Reinhart, "Penalties For Computer Hacking." *OLR Research Report*, June 28, 2012. https://www.cga.ct.gov/2012/rpt/2012-R-0254.htm.

"Are Hackers Outlaws or Watchdogs?" *PBS Frontline*. Accessed August 9, 2017. http://www.pbs.org/wgbh/pages/frontline/shows/hackers/whoare/outlaws.html.

"Hackers are not Criminals." *The Linux Geek*, May 30, 2012. http://www.thelinuxgeek.com/content/hackers-are-not-criminals.

Chris Baraniuk, "It's a Myth That Most Cybercriminals are 'sophisticated.'" *BBC Future*, July 26, 2017. http://www.bbc.com/future/story/20170726-why-most-hackers-arent-sophisticated.

Reuters, "Cyber Criminals Are Becoming Harder to Distinguish From State-Backed Hackers." *Fortune*, May 31, 2017. http://fortune.com/2017/05/31/ransomware-attack-hackers/.

"How Cybercriminals Operate." *Carnegie Cyber academy*. Accessed August 9, 2017. http://www.carnegiecyberacademy.com/facultyPages/cyberCriminals/operate.html.

W.J. Hennigan and Brian Bennett, "Criminal hackers now target hospitals, police stations and schools." *Los Angeles Times*, April 8, 2016. http://www.latimes.com/nation/la-na-0407-cyber-hospital-20160407-story.html.

Andy Orin, "Career Spotlight: What I Do as an 'Ethical Hacker.'" *Lifehacker*, May 26, 2015. http://lifehacker.com/career-spotlight-what-i-do-as-an-ethical-hacker-1706940692.

Byron Acohido, "Ethical 'white hat' hackers play vital security role." *USA Today*, November 11, 2013. https://www.usatoday.com/story/cybertruth/2013/11/11/ethical-hackers-play-vital-role-in-improiing-security/3497427/.

Arjun Kharpal, "Ethical hacking: Are companies ready?" *CNBC*, June 17, 2015. https://www.cnbc.com/2015/06/17/are-companies-still-scared-of-white-hat-hackers.html.

OPPOSING
VIEWPOINTS®
SERIES

Does the Freedom of Information Act Provide Sufficient Government Transparency?

Chapter Preface

An issue that is related to hacking, particularly in the ability to access information that the public may need to know but sources may not be willing to disclose, is the Freedom of Information Act (FOIA) and whether it provides enough access and transparency about the government. The Act, signed into law by President Lyndon B. Johnson in 1966, was intended to allow for the disclosure of information and documents controlled by the US government and which had not previously been released. It is meant to allow US citizens to request access to documents that have not already been disclosed in publicly available sources.

However, the intent of the FOIA has not always translated into the ability for citizens to access government information. The process can be difficult and access is not always granted, since the government has the discretion to decide which requests to allow and which ones are not possible for national security purposes. Many people see the FOIA as a failure, or at best, a small attempt to dispel government secrecy that is barely making a dent. However, the issue of government transparency is becoming more vital at a time when government leadership is actively attempting to prevent the release of certain types of information, even if it is scientific in nature and not overtly political.

Hacking and the FOIA are intertwined; when the FOIA process does not work, is frustratingly slow, or results in a refusal, some people may feel that hacking the government system to retrieve that same information is justified. However information is accessed, it is vitally important that US citizens should be able to access some government information if they are to be the informed citizens that an active democracy requires.

> "While open government advocates may argue over what is the best way to get more information out to the public, it seems to be universally agreed that greater proactive disclosure would be laudable."

Public Access to Government Documents Must Be Improved

Ginger McCall

Currently, accessing government documents through the FOIA requires submitting a request and then waiting for a response. In the following viewpoint, Ginger McCall argues that there are many government documents that should be posted outright online, without the necessity of a formal request. Government agencies are urged to post frequently requested documents online but do not always do so. A proactive approach to information availability, rather than a reactive one, would save time and FIA requests, the author contends. McCall litigates FOIA lawsuits for the US Department of Labor.

"How to Actually Improve Public Access to Government Documents (Under the FOIA)," by Ginger McCall, *Sunlight Foundation*, October 1, 2013. https://sunlightfoundation. com/2013/10/01/how-to-actually-improve-public-access-to-government-

As you read, consider the following questions:

1. How are investment companies using the FOIA for financial gain?
2. What is the difference between proactive and reactive disclosures?
3. Why does the author suggest a three-day delay in posting government information online?

When can a Freedom of Information Act (FOIA) request be worth millions of dollars? When it is made by an investment company hoping to gain information about potential stock purchases (and sales). A recent *Wall Street Journal* article details the use of FOIA requests by investment firms. These firms make document requests to ascertain potential corporate liabilities and successes, requesting, for example, documents detailing Food and Drug Administration inspections and customer complaints about consumer products and pharmaceuticals. To be clear, what the *Wall Street Journal* describes appears to be perfectly legal—just another form of research conducted by companies that are doing their due diligence before making large scale investments.

But it has touched a nerve within the open government community. Open government advocates argue that the investment firms are taking advantage of the FOIA in order to gain insider information that only benefits the firm and is never shared the public at large. It raises complex questions when a public interest law is used to create private gain, even though the FOIA originally accounted for commercial requesters.

Seeing potential gains in efficiency, accountability, and fairness, FOIA reformers see stories like this one as opportunities to propose new FOIA procedures to promote public access.

The first, and probably most obvious solution, is greater proactive (or affirmative) disclosure. We've written often about the benefits of proactive disclosure. Where FOIA is reactive, and necessarily limited—a person has to make an effort to draft and submit a request—proactive disclosure lowers the barrier to access by making information a mere internet search away. The President has recognized the importance of proactive disclosures and has directed agencies to "take affirmative steps to make information public" without waiting for specific requests, and, to "use modern technology to inform citizens about what is known and done by their Government." This is easiest for specific, routinely produced datasets.

The Form 483s—facility-inspection reports prepared by the Food and Drug Administration—that are the subject of the *Wall Street Journal* story would be excellent candidates for proactive disclosure. These documents are routinely produced—with around 2,500 produced last year, according to the *Journal*—and could easily be posted up online with proper redactions to protect sensitive trade secret information. This would help to level the playing field between investment companies and the public and would eliminate the time and cost associated with processing hundreds or thousands of FOIA requests for Form 483s. Handling the roughly 10,000 requests sent to the FDA in fiscal 2012 cost the government $33.5 million, and the time of more than 100 workers. The requests for Form 483s were a significant portion of these requests. The fees charged by the FDA to process requests cover only a portion of its costs.

In response to the *Wall Street Journal* story, some open government advocates have called for all FOIA responses to be posted publicly at the same time that they are given to the requester. Currently, the FOIA requires that agencies post "frequently requested" documents online. The Department of Justice has advised agencies to interpret this provision as applying to documents that are requested three or more times. Many agencies have FOIA reading rooms where such documents are posted. The problem is that not all agencies comply with this requirement, and even those that do try to comply sometimes lack the ability to keep track of how many times a document has been requested. Advocates argue that requiring agencies to post responses online

Navigating the FOIA

MuckRock, an organization designed to streamline the FOIA application process, presented "Hacking FOIA: Learn How to Open Government with Public Records" at Northeastern University on Monday. It was part of the nationwide "Sunshine Week" program to spread information about public access to government records and civic participation.

Sparsely filling up a small classroom, an audience of about 20 people, several of which are employed in media or communication fields, listened to the tips that MuckRock executive editor J. Patrick Brown offered in his half-hour presentation.

MuckRock, which partners with the *Boston Globe*'s "GlobeLab" program, follows a streamlined, three-step process: applicants put in the subject of their request, write a short description and select the level of government, such as local, state or federal, that they wish to file the request at, Brown explained.

MuckRock adds the "legalese" and takes care of the rest, "including all entanglements," from start to finish, Brown said to the audience.

Students of all majors and degree levels can use FOIA to find information about private universities through "backdoor" opportunities, or research involving both private and public universities available for public access.

In his presentation, Brown said good document requests are clearly described and defined, with clear date parameters, ideas about what agency or agent may have the information and the applicant's "status in the media," or their occupation.

Brown also recommended addressing the agent you are emailing like a "human being," and not a machine or automaton. Being direct, creative and kind may even yield faster responses, he said.

MuckRock has filed more than 30,000 requests for public records, and in total has received more than a million pages of released data since its founding in 2010, he explained.

By trying again and again, through wins and losses, MuckRock has worked to find creative ways to appeal for public release of information.

"'Hacking FOIA' Explores Requesting Public Information From Government Databases," by Megan Mulligan, *The Daily Free Press*, March 16, 2017.

after the first FOIA request would eliminate the cost of repetitively processing duplicative requests and would improve public access to government information.

The timing of the online posting, though, is a matter of debate. While some advocates have said that FOIA responses should be posted online at the same time that they are given to the requesters, others believe that a slight delay before posting online is warranted.

As a veteran FOIA requester and litigator, I see strong reasons to build in a three day delay before posting FOIA responses online. This is, by no means, the consensus around the open government community (we come from a variety of different backgrounds and sometimes do have differing opinions on how to best address policy issues). As most FOIA requesters and litigators have experienced, obtaining documents under the FOIA is a chore. Requests often take months or even years to bear fruit. And litigation takes even longer. There is often expense involved—search and duplication fees, as well as court filing fees—especially if you aren't a member of traditional media. The public interest is better served when we preserve the interest of requesters—the interest in getting an exclusive story or getting credit for fighting to make documents public. For as long as making a FOIA request takes effort, we should preserve the incentives that offset the costs of that effort. In exchange for drafting the request, hounding the agency, exhausting administrative appeals, waiting out the deadlines, and going to the trouble—and expense—of litigating, requesters should be granted few days time to review documents and write the exclusive story or take the documents to a high circulation newspaper.

In my work as a FOIA litigator, I obtained some pretty interesting documents that led to front page stories in the *New York Times* and coverage in most of the highest circulation newspapers in the country. After receiving those big envelopes (or zip file attachments) filled with documents, I would typically review the documents in the first 24 hours, work to identify the interesting parts, and then pitch them to a high circulation press outlet. Inevitably, the first question I would receive from the reporter would be "who else have you shown these documents to?" The reality of news media is that once the documents are posted online, they lose a lot of value. A set of documents that could have gotten nation-wide exposure from a paper like the *New York Times*, *Wall Street Journal*, *Washington Post*, or *USA Today*, may instead receive little or no exposure if there isn't some opportunity for short term exclusivity. If the aim is to get the information out to the largest audience, there is some value in building in a slight delay.

It is also likely that if there is no opportunity for an exclusive story, many journalists would cease to make requests and public knowledge might suffer.

Some advocates, including my own coworkers, have made principled arguments to me regarding why the information should be free and should be public immediately, but I've failed to see how a two or three day delay would, in most cases, cause a real harm to the public. If we want to combat the kind of behavior detailed by the *Wall Street Journal*, there are ways to do that. Commercial requesters are already separated out from all other requesters under the Freedom of Information Act (for fee purposes). The three day delay could be automatically waived in regards to commercial requesters. Or, all documents could be presumptively placed online, unless the requester specifically asks for a slight delay.

A three day delay before posting online would also help to address potential delays created by the practical implications of online posting. Whenever the government posts a document up online, it must comply with Section 508 Amendment to the Rehabilitation Act of 1973, a law that protects persons with disabilities. This law requires that all government documents must be machine readable. This is a fairly arduous process which might otherwise further delay the release of documents to the requester. Allowing the agency a few additional days to convert documents to machine readable format without delaying release to the requester may be an additional benefit.

These are only a few solutions that could address the problem created by investment firms exploiting government information requested under the FOIA. While open government advocates may argue over what is the best way to get more information out to the public, it seems to be universally agreed that greater proactive disclosure would be laudable, and the Form 483s would be a great place to start. Also, as agencies move their FOIA systems online, mechanisms to track and affirmatively disclose frequently requested documents should be built in.

> *"Local, state and federal agencies alike routinely blow through deadlines laid out in law or bend them to ludicrous degrees, stretching out even the simplest requests for years. And they bank on the media's depleted resources and ability to legally challenge most denials."*

The FOIA Has Excessive Accessibility Failures

ProPublica

In the following viewpoint, writers from ProPublica *argue that government delays on all levels, whether intentionally or not, have stood in the way of the accessibility of records. Several* ProPublica *reporters provide personal accounts of the various attempts they have made to access information through the FOIA, and how difficult, frustrating, and often impossible the process can be. The viewpoint excerpt chronicles two reporters who requested information, and what happened to their requests.* ProPublica *is an independent, nonprofit newsroom dedicated to exposing abuses of power by government and business.*

"Delayed, Denied, Dismissed: Failures on the FOIA Front," by *ProPublica*, Pro Publica Inc., July 21, 2016. Reprinted by permission.

As you read, consider the following questions:

1. Why would an organization like *ProPublica* especially need access to government documents or information?
2. What were some of the difficulties encountered by the organization's reporters?
3. What changes did the FOIA Improvement Act of 2016 promise?

This month marks the 50th anniversary of the Freedom of Information Act, which was designed to give the public the right to scrutinize the records of government agencies. Almost no one needs public records more than an organization like *ProPublica*, whose mission is producing work that "shines a light on exploitation of the weak by the strong and on the failures of those with power to vindicate the trust placed in them."

Yet almost every reporter on our staff can recite aneurysm-inducing tales of protracted jousting with the public records offices of government agencies. Local, state and federal agencies alike routinely blow through deadlines laid out in law or bend them to ludicrous degrees, stretching out even the simplest requests for years. And they bank on the media's depleted resources and ability to legally challenge most denials.

Many government agencies have gutted or understaffed the offices that respond to public records requests. Even when agencies aren't trying to stymie requests, waits for records now routinely last longer than most journalists can wait—or so long that the information requested is no longer useful. This, in turn, allows public agencies to control scrutiny of their operations.

There's little reason to hope things will improve. Last week, President Obama, who has repeatedly broken promises to deliver new levels of transparency, signed the FOIA Improvement Act of 2016. The act writes the presumption of disclosure clearly into law, pledges to strengthen the FOIA Ombudsman and creates a single FOIA portal for agencies to receive requests, among other user-friendly provisions. But the act explicitly provides no new resources for implementing these provisions.

To provide a sense of the difficulties encountered by *ProPublica* reporters trying to access public records, we are recounting some of our battles on the Freedom of Information front at all levels of government:

[…]

Julia Angwin

In November 2013, a U.S. customs official refused to let Toronto resident Ellen Richardson board a flight to New York because she had been hospitalized for depression—and was therefore considered a mental health risk.

A Canadian privacy commissioner investigated and found that Ontario police were routinely uploading suicide calls into a database that was accessed by the FBI and U.S. Customs and Border Patrol. And it turned out that there was an obscure provision in the immigration law that allows border agents to deny admission to people who have mental disorders that could pose a threat to themselves or others.

Curious about how many other people might have been turned away at the border on mental health grounds, I filed a FOIA on May 19, 2014 to the U.S. Citizenship and Immigration Services seeking complaints by individuals denied admission on mental health grounds as well as training manuals governing such denials and other related documents.

I heard nothing. And then, two years later, I got an email from Yael Schacher, a professor at the University of Connecticut, who said she had received my FOIA response at her home address in West Hartford.

"I opened it, thinking that the name was wrong and it was for me because, as a Harvard PhD student studying immigration, I submitted several FOIAs to USCIS in 2013 and 2014," that were

FOIA REQUESTS CAN BE PROHIBITIVELY EXPENSIVE

In Baltimore, it's recently gotten significantly more expensive to ask the police department for emails under freedom of information laws, which allow journalists and the public to request public governmental records. Here's the kicker: that change comes shortly after the release of an embarrassing email exchange revealing an officer and a prosecutor making fun of a sexual assault victim.

A journalist using MuckRock discovered the change while making an unrelated request for records. Now, two months after the embarrassing emails surfaced, it'll cost reporters and other members of the public $50 before even starting a search for emails, making "freedom" of information something of a misnomer.

MuckRock accurately describes the change as "prohibitively expensive." Freedom of information laws exist so the public can keep watch over the government and hold officials accountable. With shrinking newsroom budgets, increased concerns over libel lawsuits, and the higher cost of investigative journalism, many news outlets are finding it harder to justify important but expensive hard-hitting work. FOIA requests have resulted in some of the most significant recent news stories, including the Laquan McDonald shooting being widely publicized, CUNY being forced to reduce the salary of David Petraeus from $200,000 to $1, and an exposé of the FDA's manipulation of science journalists into providing favorable coverage, among many others.

For a functioning democracy, it's essential to invest in this type of journalism though, and government should be making this work easier, not harder.

**"Police Department Makes It 'Prohibitively Expensive' to Make FOIA Requests,"
by Ashley Dejean, Gizmodo Media Group, November 6, 2016.**

still outstanding because they had been referred to other agencies for review, Schacher wrote to me. But inside the envelope was not her FOIA response, but mine.

Kindly, she mailed the response to my office. The contents were underwhelming to say the least. The two-year wait had produced a three-page printout of an email thread, in which an immigration service employee outlined the criteria for when the agency must consult the U.S Department of Health and Human Services on mental health immigration denials.

The email answered a question I hadn't asked, and was—to be honest—beside the point.

Meanwhile, Schacher is still waiting for her FOIA. "Who knows who has received my long awaited FOIA documents!?" she wrote to me. "If you happen to get any of my documents, please send them to my home address."

Michael Grabell

Back in 2010, during the depths of the recession, the Obama administration awarded $7 billion in grants and loans to help bring high-speed internet to rural areas and inner cities. It was a key part of President Obama's $800 billion stimulus package and an endeavor often compared to the New Deal program that brought electricity to farming communities.

As part of my reporting on the stimulus for *ProPublica* and a book I was writing, I spent some time driving the unpaved back roads of rural Vermont, talking to families who were desperate for faster, more reliable connections to the outside world.

To see when, and if, they would get it, I filed a FOIA request with the U.S. Department of Agriculture in October 2010, seeking the grant applications for six of the largest projects. My goal was to see what was being promised, so that when the projects were completed, I could check if the companies—and the Obama administration—followed through.

I'm no stranger to FOIA delays.

But despite the president's pledge of unprecedented transparency with stimulus spending, I heard nothing for four-and-a-half years.

Meanwhile, construction on the broadband projects began. My book was published. And controversy grew over whether the government money was competing with private investment, whether the internet speed was fast enough, and why some communities weren't getting connected.

Finally in April 2015, the USDA sent me a letter, saying they had located approximately 4,000 pages related to my request.

But they couldn't give them to me yet. First, as is standard, they had to notify the companies behind the broadband projects to give them a chance to object to any information they might consider proprietary.

It wouldn't take much longer, the agency assured me in the letter. The companies had to respond by the end of the month.

That was the last I ever heard of my FOIA request.

Since then, much of the money has been spent. While the administration promised to connect millions of rural households, in March 2014, it lowered that number to 729,000, according to congressional investigators at the Government Accountability Office. More than 40 projects were terminated before they even began. The agency was releasing so little information, the GAO said, that it was difficult to determine if the program had worked.

"We are left with a program that spent $3 billion," a GAO investigator told *Politico* last summer, "and we really don't know what became of it."

Back in rural Vermont, a $116 million plan by VTel Wireless to bring broadband to all unserved households is officially considered complete. But the state's congressional delegation recently sent a letter to the USDA asking why they're hearing it's "only available in a few areas."

I decided to ask some local reporters how the grant application might inform their work, so I called John Lippman, who's been covering the broadband project for the *Valley News*, which covers several communities in central Vermont and New Hampshire.

To my chagrin, Lippman said he already had the grant application. He received it under FOIA last year, he said, and it took only a matter of weeks. He published a story about it.

"It was very valuable because it gave me some insight into a number of things," he said. "In the application they said they were going to be doing x, y, z. So I was able to match what they said they were going to do with how far they were in the process."

Vermont's state auditor Doug Hoffer got a copy too—but heavily redacted.

"It's a 949-page document, and 650 pages were redacted. It's a complete joke," he said. "I have to say, not only as the state auditor, but as a citizen, I'm outraged about what the U.S. Department of Agriculture agreed to in terms of redactions at the behest of the company. It's appalling. We basically were not given any information."

As I called people around Vermont, I heard back from the USDA's chief FOIA officer, who was trying to track down my request. She said it was still in process and gave me the direct number for the analyst handling my request. So I called the number and got an automated message: The number was not in service.

After I notified her, she provided the right number and, suddenly, I started receiving the applications.

I'm still waiting for two more, including a project in Western Kentucky worth more than $100 million in federal funding. But the USDA says they'll send them to me next week.

> *"Open government advocates emphasize the importance of FOIA to a fully functioning constitutional democracy."*

We Have to Keep Fighting for Freedom of Information

David L. Hudson Jr.

In the following viewpoint, David Hudson examines the history of FOIA, particularly President Lyndon B. Johnson's reluctance to sign it into law, and the tensions surrounding the FOIA still exist today. The author discusses the importance of the FOIA and why it is essential today, as well as the barriers that are still in place despite the act's very existence, and the improvements that are needed for transparency. Hudson is a regular contributor to the ABA Journal and serves as the ombudsman for the Newseum Institute's First Amendment Center.

As you read, consider the following questions:

1. Why did President Johnson have mixed feelings about signing FOIA?
2. What was John Moss's role in the passage of FOIA?
3. What are some of the challenges faced by FOIA today?

"50 Years Later, Freedom of Information Act Still Chipping Away At Government's Secretive Culture," by David L. Hudson Jr., *American Bar Association*, July 1, 2016. Reprinted by permission.

On Independence Day 50 years ago, President Lyndon Baines Johnson reluctantly signed into law the Freedom of Information Act. President Johnson thought it was terrible legislation and considered a veto after it was passed by Congress. He signed the bill into law on his Texas ranch instead of at a celebratory event at the White House.

Johnson's comments at the low-key signing ceremony at the ranch illustrated his mixed feelings about the new law. "I signed this measure with a deep sense of pride that the United States is an open society," he said. "I have always believed that freedom of information is so vital that only the national security, not the desire of public officials or private citizens, should determine when it must be restricted. At the same time, the welfare of the nation or the rights of individuals may require that some documents not be made available. As long as threats to peace exist, for example, there must be military secrets."

Johnson's comments still describe the ongoing tension between the commitment to disclosure of government information to members of the press and public measured against the governmental inclination to withhold information, most often on grounds of national security.

Consternation over FOIA was not confined to the Oval Office. More than a dozen federal agencies actively opposed the bill and testified against it at congressional hearings. But the press and some committed members of Congress actively pushed it to fruition. Even Johnson's own press secretary, Bill Moyers, encouraged his boss to sign the bill into law.

"Getting FOIA passed was almost as difficult as making it work once it was law," says Moyers, who left the administration in 1967 for a career in broadcasting and political commentary. "Even LBJ got cold feet; and only at the last minute, pressed by John Moss and his friends in the press, did he turn it around and claim FOIA as his own, even exulting over it. We had to fight for it then, and we have to keep fighting for it 50 years later."

Sharper Teeth

The concepts embodied in FOIA were not new when it became law in 1966. Provisions of the act originally were contained in the Administrative Procedure Act of 1946, but their teeth weren't very sharp. Many advocates of more open government were concerned that the APA gave federal agencies more discretion to withhold information rather than disclose it.

FOIA took those provisions out of the APA to bolster disclosure requirements governing federal agencies, and the law continues to be the leading federal statute providing a mechanism for individuals to request government documents. "The basic purpose of FOIA is to ensure an informed citizenry, vital to the functioning of a democratic society, needed to check against corruption and to hold the governors accountable to the governed," wrote Justice Thurgood Marshall in a dissenting opinion in the U.S. Supreme Court's 1978 decision in *NLRB v. Robbins Tire & Rubber Co.* that the National Labor Relations Board did not have to disclose its witness statements because they were exempt under FOIA.

Open government advocates emphasize the importance of FOIA to a fully functioning constitutional democracy. "I don't think it is possible to overstate the impact of FOIA on openness in government," says Jane E. Kirtley, director of the Silha Center for the Study of Media Ethics and Law at the University of Minnesota in Minneapolis. "The FOI Act is an imperfect tool, but as compared to many other countries' comparable legislation, it is remarkably effective. Without FOIA, we'd be left with the Administrative Procedure Act and not much else. Given the range of regulatory and enforcement activities of the executive branch, it is imperative that the public have a tool that makes it more open and accountable. FOIA is that tool."

FOIA has allowed reporters and others to uncover government abuses, wasteful government spending and safety hazards. The Sunshine in Government Initiative, a self-described "coalition of media groups committed to promoting policies that ensure the government is accessible, accountable and open," provides in its online FOIA Files numerous examples of how journalists have used FOIA requests to uncover vital information, such as how the federal government turned down millions of dollars in aid after Hurricane Katrina; how 17,000 bridges have not had up-to-date safety inspections; how there is a serious backlog of disability benefit requests that have been filed by recent veterans from wars in Afghanistan and Iraq; and how the Pentagon has ignored serious waste allegations.

"These and a long list of other such reporting never would have been possible without the FOIA," says Paul K. McMasters, a longtime advocate for the First Amendment and freedom of information who is the former national ombudsman for the Freedom Forum. "This flow of information transcends annoyances or embarrassments to public officials; it revitalizes and strengthens the working relationship between the government and the citizenry."

(As a matter of disclosure, this author holds a part-time position with the Freedom Forum as First Amendment ombudsman.)

"The federal Freedom of Information Act stands as one of the essential clauses of the working contract between a government and its citizenry," says McMasters, who is a past president of the Society of Professional Journalists. "The law assures an informed citizenry that in turn assures a government that can more effectively protect and serve that citizenry. When government officials fail, or refuse, to share with fellow citizens information vital to full and fair participation in the democratic process, however, that fragile contract is shattered. That leaves a government vulnerable to potential corruption and actual incompetence." FOIA helped change the thinking about how to approach disclosure of information by the government, says Thomas M. Susman, director of the ABA Governmental Affairs Office in Washington, D.C. "Bureaucracies are by their nature secret," says Susman. "FOIA started to reverse the culture that presumed everything was secret unless it was in the interest of the government to release it."

The Crusader

Gaining passage of FOIA was no easy thing. It took the herculean efforts of Moss, a Democratic congressman from California, to keep the measure alive for more than a decade. Moss died in 1997.

"It was an all but impossible task that took 12 years, but John Moss was tenacious and he saw it through," says Michael R. Lemov, author of *People's Warrior: John Moss and the Fight for Freedom of Information and Consumer Rights.* "President Johnson thought at one time it was terrible legislation. Presidents Truman and Eisenhower also opposed it. Every federal executive agency opposed it. John Moss is an underappreciated American hero, and he really was the people's warrior. Without his tenacious and tireless efforts, FOIA would not have been passed until much later."

Moss made his feelings clear in a speech on Capitol Hill in June 1966, shortly before his bill was passed. "We must remove every barrier to information about—and understanding of—government activities consistent with our security if the American public is to be adequately equipped to fulfill the ever more demanding role of responsible citizenship," he told his colleagues in the House.

Moss emphasized three basic changes brought about by his measure. First, the bill required that most government records would be available to "any person" rather than simply to those "properly and directly concerned." Second, the measure identified discrete categories of exempt records instead of relying on vague phrases like "good cause" or "in the public interest" to control decisions about disclosure. And third, the bill gave a person whose request for a record was denied a right to challenge that denial in federal district court.

"Everyone agrees that Moss was pivotal," says Michael S. Schudson, a professor at the Columbia Journalism School in New York City and the author of *The Rise of the Right to Know.* "He was a bulldog on the topic of freedom of information. For over a decade it was the subject he lived and breathed. He was the leader and his staff ran the switchboard connecting journalists, media lawyers and legislators to make FOIA happen."

During his tenure as speaker of the House of Representatives, Sam Rayburn appointed Moss as chairman of the Special Subcommittee on Government Information. From this position, Moss fumed that the Civil Service Commission was withholding countless documents related to the discharge of employees on the basis of security.

Moss eventually landed a co-sponsor from across the political aisle:

Donald H. Rumsfeld, an Illinois Republican who was a member of the Subcommittee on Foreign Operations and Government Information. Rumsfeld, says Schudson, "was an ardent and outspoken supporter of the legislation that became FOIA. Later, serving as secretary of defense for President George W. Bush, he was far less than a FOIA enthusiast and, in his memoir, wrote very critically of the legislation he had once supported."

A Push from the Press

FOIA was not something that sprung from public outcry over the overclassification of government documents. Moss' primary allies were journalists." The public did not insist on FOIA," Schudson says. "FOIA was generated from inside the Beltway without grassroots support. The only supporters—and they worked closely with the Moss committee—were journalists, especially organized associations of journalists like the American Society of Newspaper Editors and the journalism honorary society, Sigma Delta Chi. FOIA emerged from congressional efforts to control a rapidly growing executive branch of government, not from a general public faith in a right to know."

But FOIA was not a perfect piece of legislation. The law failed to create a culture of openness within many federal agencies. Instead, agencies often stonewalled on requests for information. Significantly, the law contained no meaningful time requirements for agencies to respond to disclosure requests.

Many government agencies broadly interpreted the nine exemptions in FOIA, covering national security, internal agency rules, the so-called statutory exemption, trade secrets, internal agency memos, personal privacy, law enforcement records, bank reports, and oil/gas well data. Some of these exemptions are still broadly interpreted by some government officials, particularly the ones addressing national security, personal privacy and law enforcement records.

In the wake of the Watergate scandal and several court decisions that expansively interpreted several FOIA exemptions, Congress amended the act in 1974. These modifications added time requirements and imposed sanctions when government officials failed to comply. Under the amendments, for instance, agencies now had 10 working days to process FOIA requests.

Citing national security concerns, President Gerald R. Ford vetoed the measure, in part based on legal advice from Antonin Scalia, who was a member of the Office of Legal Counsel. Congress overrode President Ford's veto.

"The 1974 amendments gave teeth to the law," says Susman, who was a driving force behind them as chief counsel to the Senate Subcommittee on Administrative Practice and Procedure. "Most fundamentally, it made the law much more useful to the people."

Charles N. Davis, a longtime freedom of information expert and dean of the Henry W. Grady College of Journalism and Mass Communication at the University of Georgia in Athens, says the 1974 amendments "represent the most substantive reforms to the federal act in its history." "They reflect the tumult of post-Watergate Washington and, of course, had to overcome a presidential veto—a sure sign that they were meaty enough to accomplish something. There were many substantive changes in the 1974 amendments: potential sanctions for 'arbitrary or capricious' denials of FOIA requests; uniform agency fees for search and duplication; and time limits in responding to requests. The real controversy arose over the provision calling for in camera review of requested documents by the court to see if documents were in fact properly classified."

In 1996, Congress passed the Electronic Freedom of Information Act amendments to FOIA. These clarified that electronically stored materials are records within the meaning of FOIA. Under the law, those seeking information under FOIA could request information in "any form or format" if the agency has the ability to reproduce the material in that format.

Many freedom of information experts maintain that governmental openness took a backseat during the Bush presidency, particularly after the 9/11 terrorist attacks. Nevertheless, in an address to the American Society of Newspaper Editors in 2001, Bush echoed the mixed feelings about the act that go all the way back to Johnson.

"There needs to be a balance when it comes to freedom of information laws," said Bush. "There's some things that when I discuss [them] in the privacy of the Oval Office or national security matters that just should not be in the national arena. On the other hand, my administration will cooperate fully with freedom of information requests if it doesn't jeopardize national security, for example."

When President Barack Obama took office in 2009, he pledged to provide for a more transparent government than his predecessor. In a memo to federal agencies on his first day in office, Obama wrote that "the Freedom of Information Act should be administered with a clear presumption: In the face of doubt, openness prevails."

There has been debate, however, about whether the Obama administration has followed through with the spirit of openness and transparency identified in the 2009 memorandum. "My friends involved in the access and transparency world tell me no," Susman says. "There are probably two reasons for this. First, there is the phenomenon of high expectations and lower realizations. Second, the Justice Department has been a force of restraint on agency disclosure."

Pathways Through the Forest

FOIA experts cite a number of threats to open government in the context of the act. They mention national security, privacy, the general growth in the number of classified documents and public apathy.

Schudson says both secrecy and openness have increased since the 1960s and the exponential growth of the executive branch of government. "The scope of what counts as 'national security' only grows," he says. Susman agrees: "Certainly after 9/11, national security loomed much more important. But many studies have shown that much information withheld on national security grounds would not have harmed national security if disclosed."

Kirtley says the national security exemption in FOIA remains an omnipresent threat to open government. "Trying to pry loose anything that the intelligence community considers to implicate national security is almost impossible," she says. "This is not a new problem, but I think many of us had hoped it would fade to some degree after the end of the Cold War. Unfortunately, the war on terrorism has revitalized it. Since 9/11, of course, national security in all its permutations has taken on a life of its own. The development of the concept of a sensitive, but not classified, exemption at least in practice has made it very difficult to get access to a lot of records using FOIA."

Kirtley cites privacy as another significant concern. "Many years ago, I said that privacy was going to be the biggest obstacle to successful use of FOIA," she says. "I think that is still the case. The concept of FOIA privacy has been expanded and in my opinion distorted." She cites *National Archives and Records Administration v. Favish*, a 2004 decision in which the Supreme Court broadly interpreted the personal privacy exemption in FOIA to include a right of familial privacy or survivor privacy.

"The number of classified documents grows, too," Schudson says. "At the same time, the Congress and the public have more tools for making government transparent than ever before. Picture a growing forest of secrets but also a growing number of pathways through the forest so that the keepers of secrets never know when someone might be walking his or her way through one of these growing number of and increasingly popular forest pathways."

Davis sums up the primary threat to freedom of information in one word: "apathy. The less involved people are in the functioning of government, the easier it is for governments to operate in secrecy. The diminution of the press is a massive threat to open, honest government. Where in many cities you had constant vigilance in the form of beat reporters on city and county governments, the number of boots on the ground is lower than ever; and as the ranks of reporters shrink, the sheer number of eyeballs trained on these lower levels of government—city councils, county commissions, boards of education and the numerous other institutions of local governance—grows lower and lower, and many government institutions across the country now are operating without regular attendance by the press. This terrifies me."

But while there are many threats to open government and the principle of transparency, people also are using FOIA in record numbers. The Justice Department's Office of Information Policy notes there were a record number of FOIA requests made in 2015. "These numbers are good news, but I worry about the long-haul costs of litigating denied FOIA requests in an era when the budgets of both mainstream news organizations and government watchdog organizations are strapped," says Clay Calvert, director of the Marion B. Brechner First Amendment Project at the College of Journalism and Communications at the University of Florida in Gainesville. "It's all fine and dandy to see FOIA still standing at the half-century mark with record-breaking numbers of requests, but meaningless in practice if the financial resources just aren't there to fight the time-consuming battles when those requests are denied."

Some current members of Congress have committed to improving the Freedom of Information Act. For several years, Sens. John Cornyn, R-Texas, and Patrick J. Leahy, D-Vt., have introduced the FOIA Improve-ment Act. In February, they introduced their latest version of the bill.

The measure would require federal agencies to post on their websites documents sought in at least three prior FOIA requests. The bill also would codify President Obama's memorandum of openness by establishing a default presumption of openness. Federal agencies could only deny a request under one of the law's nine exemptions if they could reasonably foresee that disclosure of the information would harm the interests protected by any of the exemptions, and they would have to explain their conclusions to those requesting disclosure.

"I strongly support this piece of legislation," says Susman. "It has many positive improvements to FOIA. The real strength of this bill is its grant of authority to the Office of Government Information Services." Under the FOIA Improvement Act, OGIS would mediate disputes between those with FOIA requests and federal agencies.

The Senate passed the measure in March. A bill is pending in the House, where passage was uncertain as of press time in early June.

"Our democracy is built upon the premise that our government should not operate in secret," Leahy says. "Fifty years ago, Congress confirmed this by passing the Freedom of Information Act, a landmark law which has brought sunshine into the halls of power and made the government more accountable to the people. As we celebrate FOIA, we must also recommit ourselves to improving it. I cannot think of a better birthday present for FOIA's golden year than Congress enacting the Senate's bipartisan FOIA Improvement Act to strengthen this treasured law and update it for the digital age."

> *"The abuse of open records law as an activists' tool wielded against researchers is prevalent enough that the Union of Concerned Scientists, a group long recognized for its hard skeptical stance on agricultural biotechnology, earlier this year published a report titled* Freedom to Bully: How Laws Intended to Free Information Are Used to Harass Researchers.*"*

Freedom of Information Is Being Used as a Tool for Harassment

Jack Payne

In the following viewpoint, Jack Payne argues that some people are using the Freedom of Information Act to apply pressure and even threaten others. The author discusses several cases of scientists who became the target of activists' requests for information. Accommodating such requests, the author argues, takes time away from scientists' valuable work. Requests for information can go further, the author contends, to the point where groups are threatening and bullying scientists into abandoning their work. While the author believes that transparency is important, he cautions against allowing such witch hunts. Payne is Senior Vice President for Agriculture and Natural Resources and Professor of Wildlife Ecology and Conservation at the University of Florida

"Activists Misuse Open Records Requests to Harass Researchers," by Jack Payne, *The Conversation*, August 27, 2015. https://theconversation.com/activists-misuse-open-records-requests-to-harass-researchers-46452. Licensed under CC-BY ND 4.0.

As you read, consider the following questions:

1. What is the connection of the viewpoint's author to Kevin Folta?
2. What is the "spiral of silence," according to the viewpoint?
3. What percentage of scientists admitted to fabricating or falsifying data, according to the meta-analysis reference in the viewpoint?

This winter, Kevin Folta, a plant molecular biologist with the University of Florida's (UF) Institute of Food and Agricultural Sciences (IFAS), became the target of a sweeping public records request from US Right to Know, an activist group that seeks to expose what it calls "the failures of the corporate food system," after answering questions on a website called GMO Answers.

Folta is chairman of the Department of Horticultural Sciences here, which I oversee as senior vice president of agriculture and natural resources at UF. His research uses genomics tools to guide traditional breeding efforts in Florida crops. On the GMO Answers site, he writes about the science of genetically modified organisms (GMOs), critically evaluating claims about the technology. He is not compensated for his time, and uses GMO Answers as a means to educate interested parties about the technology.

The result of this records request has been a months-long vetting of Folta's communications by university attorneys in preparation for handing over thousands of emails to US Right to Know. The request is also a major distraction from his work as a scientist.

In my administrative role, I have to oversee these kinds of records requests and make sure we are abiding by both the law and ethical standards of scientific research. Requests such as the one from US Right to Know consume attention and energy, pose the danger of silencing other scientists and impede us from pursuing our true mission of groundbreaking science.

"Climategate" and Misrepresented Messages

Folta is certainly not the first or only scientist to face activists bent on cherry-picking emails to distort research with a goal of applying pressure to men and women who work on controversial topics.

The most notorious case has been dubbed "Climategate," in which hackers extracted thousands of emails from the server of a British university in 2009. Climate change deniers asserted that the emails demonstrated global warming was a worldwide scientific conspiracy.

In a letter in the journal *Science*, 225 members of the US National Academy of Sciences condemned the hack as an example of "political assaults on scientists and climate scientists in particular." Scientific organizations worldwide reiterated the scientific consensus around climate change. All that, of course, could not unring the bell and put the controversy to rest.

What we've learned from episodes such as Climategate is that emails can be used out of context to confuse the public about issues around which there is, in fact, solid scientific consensus.

Open Records Requests Wielded as a Weapon

The abuse of open records law as an activists' tool wielded against researchers is prevalent enough that the Union of Concerned Scientists, a group long recognized for its hard skeptical stance on agricultural biotechnology, earlier this year published a report titled "Freedom to Bully: How Laws Intended to Free Information Are Used to Harass Researchers."

It highlights multiple cases similar to Folta's, by no means limited to agricultural biotechnology. For example:

- An occupational health scientist at West Virginia University received multiple records requests from a mining company after he investigated connections between mountaintop removal mining and adverse health effects.

- A University of North Carolina poverty researcher was targeted by a conservative think tank, requiring him to review thousands of emails.
- A legal scholar of religious freedom at the University of Virginia faced a Freedom of Information Act request backed by an LGBTQ advocacy group for phone and email records between him and various religious liberty groups.

Harassing Requests Threaten Scientific Enterprise

The expense of paper chases bothers me. What worries me more, though, is the prospect that other Kevin Foltas are silent because they do not want to be subjected to the harassment he endures. For instance, our national scientific societies have been silent during this episode.

Joy Rumble, an assistant professor of agricultural communication here at UF/IFAS, identifies this phenomenon as part of the spiral of silence. People tend not to publicly share their beliefs if they feel they're in the minority, the theory goes, for fear of isolation or reprisals. That silence feeds greater fear among dissenters as the status quo dominates the public discussion.

In a society in which the might of a megaphone too often trumps the power of ideas, self-censorship can mean truth loses.

And it's not an abstract concept to Rumble. She, too, answered a question or two on GMO Answers. She, too, was then targeted by a public records request. Her crime, in the view of the detractors who seek to discredit her, appears to be talking about talking about biotechnology. She wants to help scientists become better communicators, to bridge the gap between scientific consensus and public perception.

The Union of Concerned Scientists report decries the use of broad records requests that can hijack researchers' time, divert university money, and chill researchers' interest in communicating with the public they serve.

It's particularly distressing in an agricultural research context since 3.1 million children under the age of five die each year from malnutrition, while there are no documented cases of a child—or anyone—dying from eating GMO foods in the two decades they have been available to the public.

So when Folta gets death threats or has to deal with online posts about his deceased mother, or we have to search emails for nonexistent evidence of a conspiracy theory, that's more than a nuisance. Harassment of researchers contributes to the locking up in labs of potential solutions to worldwide problems.

Transparency Is Crucial

Yes, Folta's email communications with agricultural companies should be public records. The integrity of public university research is based in part on its transparency. It's germane that the public know where we get our funding, whatever the source.

That's different from sifting through 4,600 pages of emails and other records to mine for defamatory out-of-context sentences. Reimbursements for travel and small financial contributions to defray the cost of a conference or student attendance at a meeting are poised to be paraded as bribery-for-service.

Yet our scientific statements reflect scientific consensus and experimental evidence, not the influence of funders. While we can point to examples of cozy relationships between scientists and corporations that raise questions of research integrity, I'd argue these instances aren't the norm in the scientific community. A 2009 meta-analysis reports that 2% of scientists admit to fabricating or falsifying data. If recognized, misconduct—such as allowing results to be dictated by a funding source—can destroy careers.

For example, researcher Eric Smart was shown to have fabricated cardiovascular-diabetes data for almost a decade. Once discovered, he resigned from his position, is excluded from applying for federal grants for seven years and now teaches high school chemistry. Others typically accept settlements that demand their research be supervised or that any employers certify publications.

Such disruptions in publication and grant funding are difficult to overcome in a scientific career. Making up data is a fast track to career suicide. Researchers recognize that, and the overwhelming majority would not deliberately take that kind of risk—above and beyond what their academic integrity would dictate. Yes, it's important to acknowledge the concern that corporate funding could potentially influence or steer research in a way that falls short of falsifying data. But I have faith that the scientific enterprise self-corrects these unintentional lapses.

People opposed to this kind of harassment-via-records-request can sign the Cornell Alliance for Science #Science14 letter. It's a petition in support of academic freedom and the 14 scientists at four universities currently targeted by anti-GMO activists' public records requests.

As a university administrator, I'd rather spend money on so many things than taxpayer-funded witch hunts. We're forced to divert funds that could be used in the search to alleviate human suffering rooted in starvation and malnutrition, in producing better food with less environmental impact, and keeping our agricultural industries strong.

> *"FOIA is supposed to be about citizens having access to public documents, but only industry and special interest groups can really afford it in many cases."*

Citizens Need Easy FOIA Access to "Watch the Watchers"

Stephan Neidenbach

In the following viewpoint, Stephan Neidenbach argues that it is important to keep tabs on those groups who are applying pressure to scientists via requests for information under the Freedom of Information Act. Through his own experience of requesting information on those who have requested information on scientists, the author learns that it is not easy for individuals to obtain such material, even with FOIA on their side. He wonders if the expense and time it takes, not to mention potential harassment and threats, is worth it. Shouldn't transparency be available to individual citizens as well as well-funded groups? Stephan Neidenbach is a middle school science teacher in Annapolis, Maryland.

"Who Watches the Watchers?" My Experience with the Freedom of Information Act," by Stephan Neidenbach, *Medium*, June 29, 2017. https://medium.com/the-method/who-watches-the-watchers-my-experience-with-the-freedom-of-information-act-521c4b4cd618. Licensed under CC0 1.0.

As you read, consider the following questions:

1. Why did the viewpoint author begin submitting FOIA requests?
2. How much did some of the universities charge for emails, according to the author?
3. What nonprofit website did the author use, which helps individuals file and follow up on FOIA requests?

Almost two years ago I began submitting Freedom of Information Act (FOIA) requests on public professors that work with anti-GMO groups, the organic industry, or both. Until one such request was filed on Professor Kevin Folta due to his outspoken criticism of the anti-GMO movement, I had never heard of FOIA.

I quickly read horror stories about such requests being filed on professors who were researching evolution, climate change, and tobacco advertising to children. Emails were cherry picked in order to paint these professors in a bad light in the press. Such requests were being filed by industry and their astro-turf groups unhappy with the work being done by these professors. Just like the FOIA requests submitted on Professor Folta.

I began submitting my own for two reasons. First I wanted to expose the hypocrisy of specific professors. Charles Benbrook, Nicholas Nassim Taleb, and Hector Valenzuela have all publicly attacked Kevin Folta. So I thought it was only fair to see if they had any ties to industry of their own. But I also wanted this to be done by an individual. If a company or a pro-science NGO had submitted these requests, they would have been quickly called out in the press. But a middle school teacher with no ties to industry? What could they say about me? I am about as independent as one can get.

The request on Taleb went nowhere, he had been gone from the public university for too long. He is safe at private NYU where he can scream about transparency while not having to submit to it himself. People should take his own advice, without skin in the game can he be trusted?

Benbrook and Valenzuela were different stories. With the *New York Times* having already submitted a FOIA request on Benbrook, I wasn't expecting much. It turns out that he was selling science for $100,000:

> EXPOSURE of a private email trail has revealed one of WA organic farmer Steve Marsh's biggest backers sought to fund "scientific" research to present in a "strategic court room" as evidence of genetically modified (GM) crops being unsafe, to help demand a moratorium.
>
> Mr Kailis asked what the costs and outcomes would be of choosing the "ramrod path" of four to eight months.
>
> Dr Benbrook's reply said, "Off the top of my head, if I am the ramrod, I would need full control of process and right to be a slave driver/dictator, and at least $100k, and probably will regret promising to do it for that amount".

Valenzuela did not appear to have any such industry ties (so far), but he curiously worked hard to hide part of his emails:

> Considering the volume of information contained in the box of documents, it's totally possible that a few pages just happened to be copied in super tiny print somehow. Be it accident or clever way to foil far-sighted FOIA requesters, the MuckRock user who requested the emails, Stephan Neidenbach, has asked the University of Hawaii to re-release the illegible pages.

Upon receiving legible copies of the pages, it turned out that Valenzuela appeared to be attempting to hide misuse of university resources to harass Professor Folta:

> While free speech unfortunately often protects cyberbullying, that does not necessarily extend to public university professors using university resources. This 32 page dossier created by Valenzuela was sent to his work email from his Evernote account.

All of these revelations must have begun to upset the anti-GMO groups, as they began to attack me for using FOIA requests that they defend for their own purposes.

This of course only got me more interested. What else was going on? Why now were these preachers of transparency so worried?

More emails would reveal divisions within the anti-GMO movement and Consumers Union (while claiming unbiased independence) collaboration with extremist groups.

Some on our side were not happy with me. Professor Folta himself disagrees with me, as does David Sutherland (one of the major players behind March Against Myths). Professor Bradshaw most recently called out my FOIA requests on professors who signed a letter attacking the new pro-science film *Food Evolution*. Those professors have not even seen the film and are calling it corporate paid propaganda.

There is of course zero evidence that biotech companies had anything to do with the film. The funder, IFT, actually benefits when companies go non-GMO. Food scientists are called in to reformulate the ingredients.

But being a public middle school teacher, I have realized something. We are in the public light. The very first day I was hired, before I even knew what a GMO was, I was told to be wary of every word I put into an email. My emails were public record, no different than my curriculum or lesson plans.

One thing was still bothering me though. As an individual I cannot really afford to pay for many of those emails. Some universities have asked for upwards of $1,000. I started crowdfunding for some, but began to feel guilty about it. Shouldn't my followers donate money to vaccine charities instead?

So who watches the watchers? FOIA is supposed to be about citizens having access to public documents, but only industry and special interest groups can really afford it in many cases. I reached out to journalist Michael Morisy who started MuckRock, which allows individuals like myself to file requests. They even handle all of the follow ups for users. I asked him if FOIA is really effective if it can only be used by biased organizations and journalists at very large news organizations.

He agreed that this is a major concern, especially when countries like the United Kingdom rarely assess such fees. But he believes that "if FOIA were to go away, people who would seek to intimidate or harass simply find some new avenue to do so, while the public would lose a critical tool for democratic participation."

And on that he is 100% correct. All these groups need are insinuations and doubt. So I truly believe that someone like me is needed to step up and use the same process. Are those professors attacking *Food Evolution* over transparency really going to attack me for asking them to be transparent? The answer to that question alone may get at their true motives.

And it appears that this is happening. Already I have received an email from a Vice reporter asking about my motives. But I promise something to my followers few on either side are actually willing to. Transparency.

All of my requests and their responses are on Muckrock.com, except for a few individual cases where the university insisted on using their own electronic system. I freely admit that my first FOIA requests were a fishing expedition. I never should have requested "all" emails to or from Benbrook. I have learned from those early mistakes and now submit more specific requests.

Before all of this I once used to say about "Big Brother" that I would be fine with cameras in my bedroom, as long as we could have public cameras installed in the President's bedroom as well. Let us make sure that FOIA requests are not one sided and cherry picked. Join me. Sign up at Muckrock.com and submit one today.

The anti-science movement is going to continue no matter how much "communication" we ask of them. When everyone's dirty laundry is exposed, it just won't be a big deal anymore.

Periodical and Internet Sources Bibliography

The following articles have been selected to supplement the diverse views presented in this chapter.

Stephanie Amaru and Mark E. Elliott, "Open Wide: FOIA Reform Expands Public Access to U.S. Government Information." *Pillsbury Winthrop Shaw Pittman LLP*, July 5, 2016. http://documents.jdsupra.com/f07b1f49-6cd8-47ad-ad4d-276152aaed32.pdf.

Reema Amin, "Who uses FOIA? Journalists, lawyers, vendors and 'the average Joe.'" *The Daily Press*, May 20, 2017. http://www.dailypress.com/news/newport-news/dp-nws-nn-foia-roundup-citizens-20170520-story.html.

Ted Bridis, "Obama administration sets new record for withholding FOIA requests." *PBS.org*, March 18, 2015. http://www.pbs.org/newshour/rundown/obama-administration-sets-new-record-withholding-foia-requests/.

Michelle Cottle, "The War on the Freedom of Information Act." *The Atlantic*, July 23, 2017. https://www.theatlantic.com/politics/archive/2017/07/the-war-on-the-freedom-of-information-act/534489/.

Philip Eil, "An independent journalist explains how the Freedom of Information Act is broken." *Freedom of the Press Foundation*, March 17, 2016. https://freedom.press/news-advocacy/an-independent-journalist-explains-how-the-freedom-of-information-act-is-broken/.

Philip Eil, "MuckRock's Approach Is Working, One FOIA at a Time." *Boston Magazine*, July 3, 2016. http://www.bostonmagazine.com/news/blog/2016/07/03/muckrock-foia-turns-50/.

Philip Eil, "Six lessons from a five-year FOIA battle." *Columbia Journalism Review*, September 28, 2016. https://www.cjr.org/first_person/foia_freedom_of_information_act_doj.php.

Paul Fletcher, "Will Trump Play Nice If Journalists Launch FOIA Offensive Against His Administration?" *Forbes*, December 26, 2016. https://www.forbes.com/sites/paulfletcher/2016/12/26/will-trump-play-nice-if-journalists-launch-foia-offensive-against-his-administration/#38d6d0924d58.

"Freedom of Information Laws." *Reporter's Committee for Freedom of the Press*. Accessed August 9, 2017. https://www.rcfp.org/first-amendment-handbook/freedom-information-laws.

"The Good, the Bad, the Ugly of Using FOIA." *American Journalism review*, October 8, 2014. http://ajr.org/2014/10/08/foia-request-challenges/.

Emily Grannis, "Paying for Public Access." *Reporters Committee for Freedom of the Press*, 2014. https://www.rcfp.org/browse-media-law-resources/news-media-law/news-media-and-law-spring-2014/paying-public-access.

"History of the Freedom of Information Act." *PBS.org*, April 5, 2002. http://www.pbs.org/now/politics/foia.html.

Stephen J. Schulhofer, "Access to National Security Information under the U.S. Freedom of Information Act." *NELLCO*, May 2015. http://lsr.nellco.org/cgi/viewcontent.cgi?article=1510&context=nyu_plltwp.

For Further Discussion

Chapter 1
1. Looking at the positive and negative aspects of hacking, do you believe that it is a crime? Why or why not?
2. What effects can hacking have on corporate and government security systems?
3. How can hacking affect the average individual? Give specific examples.

Chapter 2
1. How can hacking be used as an acceptable form of civil disobedience?
2. What do you believe are the greatest risks to the political process caused by hacking?
3. Is hacking an acceptable method for ensuring government transparency? Why?

Chapter 3
1. Are all hackers breaking the law, regardless of what they do and the effects it has? Why or why not?
2. Should hacking be taught as an academic subject? How could it be incorporated into a curriculum?
3. Is the hacker code of ethics an effective way of regulating hacking? Why or why not?

Chapter 4
1. Should all government documents and information be available through the FOIA?
2. What are the problems with the current implementation of FOIA rules?
3. Why is free access to information so important in a democracy?

Organizations to Contact

The editors have compiled the following list of organizations concerned with the issues debated in this book. The descriptions are derived from materials provided by the organizations. All have publications or information available for interested readers. The list was compiled on the date of publication of the present volume; the information provided here may change. Be aware that many organizations take several weeks or longer to respond to inquiries, so allow as much time as possible.

Canadian Journalists for Free Expression

215 Spadine Avenue, Suite 162
Toronto, ON M5T 2C7 Canada
(416) 787-8156
email: cjfe@cjfe.org
website: www.cjfe.org

CJFE works to defend and protect the right to free expression in Canada and around the world. The organization champions the free expression rights of all people, and encourages and supports individuals and groups in the protection of their own and others' free expression rights.

Center for Internet Security

31 Tech Valley Drive
East Greenbush, NY 12061
(518) 266-3460
email: contact@cisecurity.org
website: www.cisecurity.org

The Center for Internet Security is a nonprofit group dedicated to safeguarding public and private organizations against cyber threats. The organization's website features detailed blogs about many facets of cybersecurity.

Electronic Privacy Information Center

1718 Connecticut Ave, N.W.
Suite 200
Washington, DC 20009
(202) 483-1140
email: info@epic.org
website: www.epic.org/

The Electronic Privacy Information Center is a public interest research center established to focus public attention on emerging privacy and civil liberties issues and to protect privacy, freedom of expression, and democratic values in the information age.

Information Systems Security Association

11130 Sunrise Valley Drive, Suite 350
Reston, VA 20191
(703) 234 4077
website: www.issa.org/

The Information Systems Security Association is a professional association of cybersecurity professionals, promoting effective cyber security and providing education and knowledge.

MuckRock

website: www.muckrock.com/

MuckRock is a non-profit, collaborative news site that brings together journalists, researchers, activists, and regular citizens to request, analyze, and share government documents, making politics more transparent and democracies more informed. The site provides a repository of hundreds of thousands of pages of original government materials, information on how to file requests, and tools to make the requesting process easier.

The National Archives and Records Administration

8601 Adelphi Road
College Park, MD 20740-6001
(866) 272-6272
website: www.archives.gov/ogis

The National Archives Office of Government Information Services (OGIS) is a Freedom of Information Act (FOIA) resource for the public and the government. It reviews FOIA policies, procedures and compliance of federal agencies and identifying ways to improve compliance.

National Cyber Security Alliance

1010 Vermont Ave NW, Suite 821
Washington, D.C. 20005
202-570-7430
email: info@staysafeonline.org
website: https://staysafeonline.org/

The National Cyber Security Alliance and its project Stay Safe Online were developed to educate and empower the global digital society to use the internet safely and securely.

Project On Government Oversight

1100 G Street, NW, Suite 500
Washington, DC 20005
(202) 347-1122
email: info@pogo.org
website: www.pogo.org/

POGO is a nonpartisan independent watchdog group that investigates corruption, misconduct, and conflicts of interest to achieve a more effective, accountable, open, and ethical federal government.

Reporters Without Borders for Freedom of Information

Washington, DC
(202) 204-5554
email: dcdesk@rsf.org
website: https://rsf.org/en/us-chapter

Reporters Without Borders, or Reporters Sans Frontières, is an international non-profit, non-governmental organization that promotes and defends freedom of information and freedom of the press.

Society of Professional Journalists

Eugene S. Pulliam National Journalism Center
3909 N. Meridian St.
Indianapolis, IN 46208
(317) 927-8000
website: www.spj.org/foi.asp

SPJ is an organization dedicated to promoting journalism and protecting a free press.

WikiLeaks

Box 4080
University of Melbourne
Victoria 3052
Australia
email: wl-usa@sunshinepress.org
website: https://wikileaks.org/

WikiLeaks specializes in the analysis and publication of censored or otherwise restricted official materials involving war, spying and corruption.

Bibliography of Books

John Allen. *Online Privacy and Hacking*. San Diego, CA: ReferencePoint Press, 2013.

Richard A. Clarke. *Cyber War: The Next Threat to National Security and What to Do About It*. New York, NY: Ecco, 2012.

Gabriella Coleman. *Hacker, Hoaxer, Whistleblower, Spy: The Many Faces of Anonymous*. New York, NY: Verso, 2015.

John Covaleski. *Hacking*. San Diego, CA: ReferencePoint Press, 2013.

Susan Dudley Gold. *Freedom of Information Act*. New York, NY: Cavendish Square Publishing, 2011.

Marc Goodman. *Future Crimes: Inside the Digital Underground and the Battle for Our Connected World*. New York, NY: Anchor Books, 2016.

Kerry Hinton. *Hackathons*. New York, NY: Rosen Publishing, 2017.

Phill Jones. *Freedom of Information*. New York, NY: Chelsea House, 2012.

Fred Kaplan. *Dark Territory: The Secret History of Cyber War*. New York, NY: Simon & Schuster, 2017.

Brian W. Kernighan. *Understanding the Digital World: What You Need to Know about Computers, the Internet, Privacy, and Security*. Princeton, NJ: Princeton University Press, 2017.

Brian Krebs. *Spam Nation: The Inside Story of Organized Cybercrime-from Global Epidemic to Your Front Door*. New York, NY: Sourcebooks, 2015.

Steven Levy. *Hackers: Heroes of the Computer Revolution*. New York, NY: O'Reilly Media, 2010.

Raef Meeuwisse. *Cybersecurity for Beginners*, 2nd edition. London, England: Cyber Simplicity Ltd., 2017.

Raef Meeuwisse. *The Cybersecurity to English Dictionary*. London, England: Cyber Simplicity Ltd., 2017.

Kevin Mitnick. *Ghost in the Wires: My Adventures as the World's Most Wanted Hacker*. New York, NY: Back Bay Books, 2012.

Patricia D. Netzley. *How Serious a Problem Is Computer Hacking?* San Diego, CA: ReferencePoint Press, 2014.

Parmy Olson. *We Are Anonymous: Inside the Hacker World of LulzSec, Anonymous, and the Global Cyber Insurgency.* New York, NY: Back Bay Books, 2013.

Jason Porterfield. *White and Black Hat Hackers.* New York, NY: Rosen Publishing, 2017.

Kevin Poulsen. *Kingpin: How One Hacker Took Over the Billion-Dollar Cybercrime Underground.* New York, NY: Broadway Books, 2012.

Daniel Regalado, et al. *Gray Hat Hacking: The Ethical Hacker's Handbook*, Fourth Edition. New York, NY: McGraw-Hill Education, 2015.

P. W. Singer. *Cybersecurity and Cyberwar: What Everyone Needs to Know.* New York, NY: Oxford University Press, 2014.

Jonathan Smith. *White Hack Hacking.* New York, NY: Cavendish Square, 2015.

Ben Worthy. *The Politics of Freedom of Information: How and Why Governments Pass Laws that Threaten their Power.* Manchester, England: Manchester University Press, 2017.

Index